John Markham's COLOURFUL CHARACTERS

Foreword
by
Roy Woodcock

Highgate Publications (Beverley) Limited, 1992

British Library Cataloguing in Publication Data

Markham, John
 John Markham's Colourful Characters
 I. Title
 942.830099

ISBN 0-948929-59-6

Published by Highgate Publications (Beverley) Ltd.
24 Wylies Road, Beverley, North Humberside, HU17 7AP.
Telephone (0482) 866826

Printed and Typeset in 10 on 11pt Bembo by
Colourspec, Unit 7, Tokenspire Park, Hull Road,
Woodmansey, Beverley, HU17 0TB.
Telephone (0482) 864264

© John Markham, 1992

Illustrations — Acknowledgements
 John Markham gratefully acknowledges the assistance of the following who have generously provided illustrations in their ownership and given permission for their reproduction: Mr. Martin Craven, Dr. Kenneth Green, Hull City Museums and Art Galleries, Humberside Leisure Services, Hymers College, Leeds City Council, Department of Leisure: Libraries, National Portrait Gallery, London, Dr. David Neave, North Holderness Museum of Village Life, Hornsea, Mrs. J. Skowronek, Mr. Peter Walker, Mr. Tony Wharton, and his colleague, Martyn Kirby, who gave considerable help with photographs.
 If he has omitted to thank anyone for such assistance with illustrations he humbly apologises.

Contents

	Page
Foreword	iv
Preface	v
Dr. John Alderson — Doctor and Intellectual Leader	1
Henry Blundell — Manufacturer and Reformer	7
Daniel Boyes — Publican and 'Prime Minister of Beverley'	13
Cuthbert Brodrick — Hull Architect of Genius	16
Rose Carr — The Superwoman Carrier of Hornsea	22
John Edward Champney and William Spencer — Creators of the Beverley Library	25
Madame Clapham — Society Dressmaker	29
Rev. Joseph Coltman — Clergyman and Public Benefactor	35
Sir Thomas Aston Clifford Constable — A Young Man of Privilege	38
William Constable — Shoemaker and Practical Joker	43
William Crosskill — Beverley's Pioneer of Engineering	46
Thomas Robinson Ferens — Businessman and Benefactor	50
(William) Alfred Gelder — Architect and Civic Leader	55
Charles Greenwood — Landlord of the Tiger Inn, Beverley	59
Joseph Hind — Radical Councillor and Controversialist	63
James Weir Hogg — Free-spending M.P. for Beverley	66
Joseph Malet Lambert — Clergyman, Social Reformer and Pioneer of Education	69
William Middleton — Builder of Georgian Beverley	72
James Craig Niven — Botanist and Garden Designer	76
Zachariah Charles Pearson — Shipowner and Public Benefactor	80
George Frederick Samuel Robinson, Earl de Grey and Ripon — Unseated M.P. and High Steward of Hull	83
Dr. Thomas Sandwith — Doctor and Public Servant	88
Daniel Sykes — The Reluctant M.P. for Hull and Beverley	91
Thomas Perronet Thompson — Hull's brilliant but flawed M.P.	95
Admiral Charles Francis Walker — Naval Hero and Beverley Benefactor	99
Charles Henry Wilson, Lord Nunburnholme — Shipping Magnate and Liberal M.P.	102

Foreword

I was delighted to be asked to contribute a foreword to this book, because John Markham's *Colourful Characters* have been gracing the pages of various editions of the *Target* Series of weekly newspapers since they were launched under my editorship some three years ago.

The articles have proved immensely popular and I know from the response we received that this book, preserving some of the articles in more permanent form, will be welcomed by our readers and a whole new audience in areas of the East Riding that we do not reach.

Some of the earliest articles contributed by John were printed in the Hull editions of the *Target* just after we launched the papers. The launch coincided with our move to Blundell's Corner in Hull and, among others, John appropriately told the fascinating story of the man behind that name: Henry Blundell.

John followed up that series with similar ones in the *Beverley Target*, the *Holderness Target* and, this year, the recently relaunched *Beverley Advertiser*, which became part of the *Target* Series in July.

Blundell, along with people such as William Constable, Rose Carr, Alfred Gelder, Thomas Ferens and Admiral Walker, was certainly a colourful character, and they can all be found within the pages of this fascinating volume.

The hallmark of John Markham's writing is the thoroughness of the research coupled with a storytelling style that makes his subjects come alive again. This is an object lesson in making history interesting even to the most casual reader.

That this area has no shortage of colourful characters is obvious. John seemingly has a bottomless pit of subjects, some known, some less well known to the general public. What is certain is that through his writing we are able to understand our heritage that much better.

In the same way that many will have eagerly awaited publication of this book I too await further writings from John which I'm sure will grace the pages of the *Target* Series and *Beverley Advertiser* again in the future.

ROY WOODCOCK
Editor, *Target* Series of Newspapers

Preface

The personalities of Victorian and Edwardian England have great appeal today — not merely the nationally famous figures but, even more strongly, the men and women who left their mark on the town or village where they lived or worked.

Finding a reason for this interest is not difficult. These were people who had the courage to be themselves and made no attempt to assume a false face. They totally ignored anything others might think or say about them.

There were fewer bureaucratic restrictions then to constrain a forceful personality, and inhabitants of the more circumscribed, greyer modern world have reason to envy those who rose sublimely over both circumstances and public opinion.

Of course, it is never as simple as it sounds. In any age it is easier to be eccentric if you are financially independent, and most of the characters whose stories are told in this book had the advantage of an assured income, or, at the least, of self-employment. There were no multi-nationals, and even the large firms were relatively small by modern standards.

It was also easier in the Victorian and Edwardian periods to earn a reputation as a character. There were no media personalities, no hyped celebrities with whom to compete, and the mannerisms and sayings of shopkeepers, schoolteachers and businessmen made a powerful impact on their communities and soon became part of local mythology. It was probably just as satisfying being a big fish in a small pond as it would be now featuring in the tabloids as an international jet-setter.

History is much more enjoyable when it is studied through people rather than through statistics, but there is a danger in seeing people of the past as funny characters who behaved quite differently from ourselves. Such a distorting approach results in bad history, but it is dangerously easy to present a picture of a person which no contemporary would ever have recognised.

Another temptation for a writer is to see the past through rose-tinted spectacles and, in the pages of a book, to transform people one would have hated in reality into amusing characters. Distance lends enchantment to the view and some are more attractive after death than they ever were in life.

If I have committed any of these faults, this does not mean that I am unaware of the problems or have made no attempt to avoid them.

The vast majority of these chapters have appeared as articles in *Hull Daily Mail* publications, and I am grateful to Roy Woodcock, editor of the *Target* newspapers and the *Beverley Advertiser*, and Keith Perry, editor of *The Journal*, for their co-operation in the production of this book.

The word 'colourful' in the title has been interpreted very loosely. Some of the characters were more extrovert than others who qualify for inclusion because they left a distinctive imprint on local history. Whatever their differences, they have one thing in common. They all interest me, and will, I hope, interest those who read about them.

JOHN MARKHAM

Dr. John Alderson
(1757-1829)
Doctor and Intellectual Leader

John Alderson is one of my heroes — a man of many talents who pursued a busy medical practice but still found time for a formidable round of public service. As far as I am concerned, his obstinacy and occasional outbursts of temper only make him a more likeable person.

Dr. John Alderson's statue in front of Hull Royal Infirmary rarely receives more than a passing glance from people using the car park, often too pre-occupied by more immediate worries to wonder who he was. Yet it stands in the right place, for Alderson was in his day Hull's most eminent doctor, closely associated with the town's first infirmary, and an illustrious link between past and present.

John Alderson came to Hull only by chance. He was born in Lowestoft c.1757, the son of a Nonconformist minister. Appointed surgeon to the Norfolk Militia, he naturally accompanied his regiment to Hull when it was stationed on the east coast in the 1780s, a time when England was at war with France and invasion seemed imminent. Apart from a brief period in Whitby, he remained in Hull for the rest of his life.

Obviously something about the town fired his imagination. He had arrived in Hull during an exciting period in its history. The old walls had been demolished and the first dock (Queen's Dock) opened in 1778. Trade was flourishing and during Alderson's lifetime two more docks were built to encircle the town. Hull was prospering and its confidence and optimism were high. It was also becoming a smart place with fine new streets of elegant houses in its Georgian suburbs. There was no reason whatever for John Alderson to feel that he had buried himself alive in a backwater. Progress was in the air and he was determined that Hull should have its rightful place among the country's leading towns.

Dr. Alderson was consulted by many prominent people in Hull and district, among them the wife and daughters of Thomas Thompson M.P., the banker and merchant who built Cottingham Castle. But it was his work for the ordinary people which brought him gratitude and fame. From 1792 to his death in 1829 he was honorary physician at the Infirmary opened in 1784 in Prospect Street (now the site of the

Dr. John Alderson's statue in the City Hall, formerly in the Mechanics Institute.

Prospect Centre). This was a period when smallpox was one of the diseases which ravaged the population and one of Dr. Alderson's many public-spirited acts was the offer he made in 1802 to vaccinate all poor persons with pure cowpox at his surgery, free of charge.

He was a man with a strong sense of duty. Although his professional workload was onerous, he voluntarily devoted half his time to activities which would benefit the community. Alderson was determined that Hull should be a town where culture flourished and he saw material prosperity as the ally, not the enemy, of a civilised way of life. Wealth, in his view, provided the resources to enable people to live in agreeable surroundings and develop their intellectual interests. When in 1801 he laid the foundation stone of the new premises of the Hull Subscription Library in Parliament Street he stated his conviction that commerce and literature had always gone hand in hand. 'Literature,' he said, 'is indispensable to the happiness and prosperity of a commercial town.'

Alderson was not a remote academic, content to follow self-satisfying pursuits in the privileged seclusion of his own study. He realised the benefits which practical knowledge could bring, and in 1804 he proposed a series of annual lectures 'on such subjects as might be most usefully applied to the commercial and agricultural interests of the town and neighbourhood'.

Although men of his time and social status had servants to relieve them of many of the routine tasks which eat away the hours of people in similar positions today, one can nevertheless only wonder at the quantity of work John Alderson managed to complete. Every minute seems to have been spent on some worthwhile activity. In 1822 he became the first president of the Hull Literary and Philosophical Society and the progress it made during his four-year period in office owed much to his energetic example.

A powerful motivating force of men like Alderson was religion. He believed that one day he would have to account for the use he had made of his talents, his time and his privileges. Helping the less fortunate was an important part of his community role and it was only to be expected that he should be one of the main promoters of the Mechanics Institute, an organisation for adult education among the working classes, opened in Hull in 1825.

In a busy life he somehow found the time — and energy — to deliver a number of important lectures, and the learned papers he wrote indicate the wide field of knowledge over which his enquiring mind ranged. His impressive list of publications includes essays on contagious fever, on improving poor soil, on the geology of Hull and its neighbourhood, and even one on apparitions, based on his experience of patients suffering from mental illness.

No one is perfect. He did not like his opinions to be contradicted, and

Dr. and Mrs. J. A. R. Bickford, historians of the Hull medical profession, have given an assessment of his character and reputation which is both concise and fair: 'Occasionally hot-tempered and obstinate in argument, he was,' they write, 'nevertheless held in esteem by his colleagues and great affection by his fellow townsmen.'

As a man of science Alderson was in the forefront of the campaign to improve medical education so that local doctors were kept up-to-date with the findings of research and able to devise treatment on the secure basis of logic and fact rather than the unproven theories which had often been their guide in the past. There was still a long way to go before the expertise of modern medicine was achieved, but from 1825 Alderson and the staff of the Infirmary were performing valuable pioneering service by giving lectures to all the town's medical apprentices.

Sadly, he did not live to see the opening in 1831 of the institution he had helped to establish, the Hull and East Riding School of Medicine and Anatomy, in a room in Charles Street which he had given. The school moved in 1833 to its new purpose-built premises in Kingston Square and it was fitting that his doctor son, James, should have had the honour of delivering the first lecture. Until its closure in 1869 medical students could receive their training in Hull. Now the building has been

Medical School, Kingston Square, opened 1833, closed 1869, later the Blind Institute and the Co-operative Institute.

demolished, apart from the façade which remains as a further reminder of this golden age of intellectual activity in Hull.

James Alderson is the most famous member of John's family. John Alderson had married Sarah Isabella Scott, but even affluent families were steeled to a succession of children dying in infancy. The Aldersons were no exception. Five daughters and a son all died young, though a further four sons and one daughter survived. The daughter, Margaret, married John Vincent Thompson, son of Thomas Thompson M.P. and brother of Thomas Perronet Thompson.

James had a distinguished career at Cambridge, started a practice in London, but returned to Hull when his father died in 1829 and until 1841 followed in his footsteps as honorary physician at the Infirmary. He lived for a time in Albion House, Albion Street (later more famous as the premises of the Church Institute, now a hotel), but moved back to London and became senior physician at St. Mary's Hospital. As one of the country's leading doctors he was elected president of the Royal College of Physicians, and a Fellow of the Royal Society. For his services as a physician to Queen Victoria he was knighted.

In addition to the familiar statue on Anlaby Road (erected by public subscription and costing £300) which originally stood in front of the old Infirmary in Prospect Street, John Alderson is commemorated in Hull

Albion House, residence of Dr. James Alderson for a short time in the 1840s, later Church Institute.

(Martyn Kirby)

by a portrait in Wilberforce House, by a graceful memorial in Holy Trinity Church, and by another lesser known but finer statue by the distinguished sculptor Thomas Earle in the foyer of the City Hall, depicting him as a toga-clad Roman. It was formerly in the Mechanics Institute in Charlotte Street, whose foundation stone he had laid a short time before his death. A brass tablet on its pedestal carries a lengthy inscription which includes two sentences: 'As a man and a gentleman, a member of society his career was marked by all the features which distinguish the advocate of virtue and the well being of the human race. Humane and benevolent without distinction of sect or party, he was active in promoting every object which promised general good, whether it assumed the shape of scientific and literary association or societies for the prevention and relief of distress.'

Epitaphs and obituaries are not always to be trusted but this is one which really means what it says.

Dr. John Alderson's statue outside Hull Royal Infirmary, formerly in Prospect Street.

Henry Blundell
(1789 — 1865)
Manufacturer and Reformer

I have been accused of idealising some 19th-century characters, but I still think that men like Henry Blundell were about as good as anyone can be expected to be. Like John Alderson, he had his faults, but they only make him a more credible and understandable human being.

Mention Blundell's Corner in Hull any time during the last hundred years and immediately everyone knows you mean the place where Spring Bank meets Beverley Road. Older people now recall the days when this was the site of a factory and its chimney a local landmark. Some remember, too, the First World War, when Blundell's buzzer warned of a Zeppelin raid.

The man who gave his name to Blundell's Corner, however, is usually forgotten — quite wrongly, because he was one of Hull's larger-than-life figures who did far more for the town than many whose fame has lasted longer.

Henry Blundell, born in 1789 in Lincoln, began his career as an apprentice to Piercy and Thomas, brushmakers, of Church Street. He set up as a brushmaker in Hodgson Street in 1810, and a year later entered into a partnership with his brother-in-law, William Spence. Together they went into business as colour and paint manufacturers.

By the mid-19th century he had risen through the ranks to become 'the chief among our merchant princes'. The story of his self-made success was one the Victorians loved to tell their children as a moral lesson on the earthly rewards of plain living and hard work. In his case it happened to be true.

Blundell was the exact opposite of Zachariah Pearson — a man prepared to take massive risks who in a single day lost his entire fortune through a fatal error. Instead, *he* built on solid foundations, developing his knowledge of machinery and chemistry and devising new methods of paint manufacture which were to give his products an international reputation: 'Toil, patient, plodding, untiring toil, ingeniously directed and hopefully endured, has been the secret of his success.'

Henry Blundell was a man of his time, in his element in a period when Britain led the world in a dazzling display of inventive genius, and

Henry Blundell

(Dr. Kenneth Green)

when one could still be enraptured by the romance of industrial progress. Henry Blundell, an ecstatic journalist wrote, 'made dull earths and mineral poisons to give out and yield up to him colours as various and as rich as those of the solar rainbow'. A more mundane but useful achievement was his invention of an improved hydraulic press for oil extraction. The same writer, who obviously knew Blundell well, described him as 'a man of exceptional energy with his shirt sleeves rolled up, sketching out a new crank or cog-wheel, of special adaptation to his works'. His business grew, but for years he was content to live like any of his workmen in a cottage on Beverley Road in front of the factory.

Blundell's Corner, 1884.

Blundell, according to reliable evidence, was utterly unlike the tyrannical 19th-century factory owners who over-worked and underpaid their wretched employees. His company was very much a family firm run on paternalistic principles which would probably be unacceptable today but which had obvious attractions for employees of that period: 'A situation in any department of Mr. Blundell's works was the ambition of many a working man.' Sons followed fathers into the firm where Henry Blundell regarded old employees as friends: there were no state pensions then and a high compliment was intended when it was noted that 'No man in Hull has in his service so many grey-headed old servants.' Tangible expressions of the regard reciprocated by his workforce was their presentation to him in 1856 of a silver stand with golden pen holder and pen 'as a mark of esteem for his uniform kindness and liberality'.

By mid-century Blundell was one of Hull's major employers, a force in its economy, spending the enormous sum of £1,000 a week in the town on wages and purchases. Equipment was all first-class and Blundell's Corner looked 'more like a small town, or a cluster of separate manufacturing properties than the possessions of one firm'. He expanded into a modern mill in Wincolmlee (his initials, 'HB', are still there on the end plates of tie rods), he opened fine new premises in London, and his salesmen were regular visitors to the United States and Europe.

Outside business he took a leading role in public affairs, particularly as a prominent Liberal member of Hull Town Council, to which he was first elected as the representative for Myton ward in the reformed Corporation which began life in 1836. He was immediately elevated to the rank of alderman. In 1852 he became mayor. Blundell's guiding principle was reform and he was ready to shoulder any upopularity his policies produced, not least his enthusiasm for improved sanitation, crucially important but criticised on account of its cost. In a magnificent gesture he responded by asking that his own premises should be highly rated so that he could bear his full share of the burden.

Rightly convinced of the benefits free trade would bring the port, he was an influential Liberal campaigner in parliamentary elections and there were those who thought *he* was the man who should have been a Hull M.P. himself.

Victorian biographers were so prone to overload their subjects with praise that they tended to transform them into incredible paragons of virtue, far too good to be true. Henry Blundell, like every human being, had his faults, but the criticisms levelled at him by the writer who also bestowed the praise suggest that the compliments were more likely to be genuine. He was the kindly, father-figure to his employees but, quick-tempered, 'snappish and impatient' with his council colleagues.

He demeaned himself by driving a hard bargain when the Corporation wanted to acquire some of his property for improving the atrocious conditions in Wincolmlee, and, it was alleged, he ruined Spring Bank's appearance as an attractive promenade by extending a new warehouse to the very edge of his land. Blundell's Corner was not universally popular: 'The model boulevard has ceased to be a model and has a half-suffocated look, garrotted as it is by the incubus of brickwork which Mr. Blundell has so needlessly placed on its throat.'

Eventually he had moved to a grander residence, built 1827-8 to his own design, not far from his factory on Beverley Road. Brunswick House (commemorated in the name of Brunswick Avenue) was 'a handsome square building' approached by a flight of stairs, with spacious rooms and a fine garden containing a greenhouse, hot houses and an ice house. At Brunswick House in 1863 the Earl de Grey and Ripon, High Steward of Hull, 'condescendingly sat' to have his photograph taken after the unveiling of the statue of Queen Victoria in Pearson Park.

The passing of a great man was the opportunity for a Victorian journalist to play upon the emotions of his readers and remind them of their own mortality. In 1865 Blundell, a tolerant Unitarian, had contributed generously towards a gift which he was to present on behalf of the congregation to a departing Minister of the Bowlalley Lane Chapel. He developed a bronchial cold and died before the ceremony could take place. 'Many an eye,' it was claimed without exaggeration, 'will have dimmed with heartfelt sorrow for the loss of one whose great study in life was how he could best assist in alleviating the distress of the destitute poor of all creeds and of all shades of opinion.'

In appearance, Henry Blundell was remarkably fair with 'sharp, angular features'. His hair had grown silver with age and his mouth twitched continually with barely suppressed nervous energy. All the more pity, therefore, that his bust now in the foyer of the Guildhall (and originally in the Victorian Town Hall) fails to reflect his personality, even though it was the work of an eminent sculptor, W. D. Keyworth snr. The circumstances in which it was created provide the explanation: Keyworth worked from Blundell's death mask.

In spite of its aesthetic defects, however, it is a moving symbol of everything for which he had striven, for it was given in tribute by the working men of Hull. It deserves a respectful glance from their descendants whenever they pass by.

Blundell's Corner today, headquarters of the Hull Daily Mail and its associated publications. (Martyn Kirby)

Daniel Boyes
(1804-73)
Publican and 'Prime Minister' of Beverley

Daniel is one of the great characters of 19th-century Beverley. Some of his activities were outside the law, but he brought great colour into the community. After all the horrors of the 20th century his wrongdoings seem very trivial.

The Angel, Butcher Row, had a remarkable 19th-century landlord, Daniel Boyes, who played a major role in the life of the town. When he died in 1873, the *Beverley Recorder* asked rhetorically 'if there has ever lived in the borough one more noted'.

Born in 1804, he served an apprenticeship as a glazier and was landlord of the Valiant Soldier before moving to The Angel in the 1840s. It was then only a modest, low building, according to an old Beverley man who remembered it, but in Boyes' time, about 1850, the present inn was built. Traces of the old structure remain, though oddly, it seems that The Angel never had cellars, usually the feature which survives all alterations.

Daniel Boyes was no shrinking violet (though so far no portrait or photograph of him has been discovered) and as skilful in creating publicity for The Angel as any modern public relations officer. A brilliant ploy was to invent an instant tradition: New Year's Day would be celebrated at The Angel by the baking of an enormous game pie for the enjoyment of his customers. In 1841, the *Hull Advertiser* reported, it weighed more than seven stone, and, in the mannered style to which journalists then aspired, commented that 'the pastry cook had evidently exercised her best skill in (its) formation, and the great number who afterwards partook left substantial token that it was good and pleasant to the taste'. Three years later it had increased tremendously in size and so had the statistics beloved by Victorians. It was now 10 stone, 18 inches wide, 12 inches high, and 2 feet 2 inches long, enabling 35 persons each to take 'a thumping slice'.

But it was Daniel's political activities which made him an important figure in the town and The Angel a centre of activity. He was a power in the local Liberal party, a leading councillor for many years, and the inn became the meeting place for councillor colleagues and like-minded friends. In Council meetings he was admired by his supporters

The Angel Hotel, Butcher Row, Beverley, rebuilt c.1850.

for 'his coolness under debate and his consummate tact in dealing with his opponents'.

He was particularly energetic as an organiser of the campaigns of parliamentary candidates in a period when Beverley was notorious for its corrupt elections. Years later, and with surprisingly vague memory, he agreed, rather reluctantly, that 'it might have happened' that money had been left at The Angel to pay voters' expenses. The power he wielded was so great that he earned himself the title of 'Prime Minister of Beverley' and bribery was no barrier to his popularity in Beverley — rather the reverse.

After the 1859 election Daniel was summoned to London to give evidence before the House of Commons committee which, at the conclusion of the hearing, unseated the recently elected M.P. for whom he had campaigned and recommended that criminal proceedings be started against Daniel himself. He returned to Beverley to a hero's welcome. It was after midnight, but a torchlight procession headed by a band heralded his arrival at the railway station and accompanied him in his triumphal progress to The Angel, the greater portion of his admirers being females in a half-dressed state.

He was a fearless, controversial debater, often in hot water. In June, 1855, a newspaper report began in a way which sounds strangely modern: 'On Saturday night last the town of Beverley was in a state of commotion.' Daniel had made some provocative remarks about billeting to which the militia took exception, and The Angel had to be defended against a military attack. In a heated election row years later, over a hundred men armed with sticks, staves and chair legs went to the front of The Angel and, when Daniel appeared, he was attacked 'in a most shameful manner. Sticks, *etc.* were thrown at him and one man hit him over the head with a rail.'

He managed to wear a remarkable number of hats; one was that of Secretary to the Race Committee, and on display in The Angel today is a poster for the Easter races of 1870. All entries had to be made to him at The Angel, and stakes were paid out there to winners in the evening following the races — a subtle way of increasing trade.

His last years were a sad final chapter of declining health and he had to retire from the public activities which to him had been the stuff of life. When he died in 1873 he was already a man of the past. Beverley, too, was changing. The town had lost its right to parliamentary representation because of its shameful record, the introduction of the secret ballot a year earlier was a major factor ending bribery, and the old-style elections were passing into history.

For Daniel none of these changes was for the better.

Cuthbert Brodrick
(1822-1905)
Hull Architect of Genius

People whose lives contain an element of mystery are far more intriguing than those who behaved in a totally predictable way. Brodrick had a brilliant start to his architectural career, but why did he give it all up at the peak of his fame?

'Yuppies' attract, and probably deserve, contempt, but it is sometimes forgotten that many famous Victorians whose heavily-bearded visages suggest they were bowed down with years were quite young men. Cuthbert Brodrick, an architect of remarkable talent, born into a Hull shipping family in 1822, completed his articles to another distinguished architect, H. F. Lockwood, in 1843, travelled abroad looking at fine examples of European architecture which were to have a profound influence on his career, and in 1852, when he was only 30, successfully submitted plans for a building in Albion Street, Hull, to be used by the Literary and Philosophical Society and the Subscription Library.

One secret of success is to be in the right place at the right time and to have the vision and ability to exploit one's opportunities. As a Yorkshireman, Brodrick was fortunate that this was a time when northern towns were growing in wealth and importance through commerce and industry. Local men were determined to have buildings as grand as any in London, certainly not inferior to those in a rival town. Cuthbert Brodrick, who had seen the impressive buildings of Continental cities and was a great admirer of classical architecture, was the one to fulfil their ambitions.

His first major commission in Hull, the 'handsome edifice' in Albion Street, became the Royal Institution when it was visited by the Prince Consort on 14 October, 1854. Ten days later it was formally opened, 'a credit to, and one of the chief ornaments, of the town', with great Corinthian columns adding grandeur to its façade. The interior was no anti-climax: lofty chambers with ultramarine ceilings were embellished with pillars and pilasters painted to resemble green marble and red granite, their white capitals edged with gold. All one can do now is read descriptions. On the night of 24 June, 1943, by which time it had become the Municipal Museum, it was destroyed in an air raid, and a

Cuthbert Brodrick.

Cupola of the Victorian Town Hall, now in Pearson Park.

Christ Church School, Kingston Square, Hull, 1849.

Cuthbert Brodrick's Town Hall, opened 1866, demolished 1912.

major part of the life work of Curator Tom Sheppard, 'The Great Collector', was ruined.

Victorian buildings are so often the outward and visible expression of the confidence, pride and optimism of their founders, and the town halls of the North of England embodied the attributes and attitudes of the leaders of the community.

Leeds was well aware of what was happening in Bradford, and the building of St. George's Hall was the spur to produce something even better. It was decided to have a new town hall, and Sir Charles Barry, architect of the House of Commons, acted as adviser in a competition to find a suitable design. In spite of the qualms of some councillors about his youth, Brodrick was awarded the first prize of £200 and entrusted with the commission.

Park House was purchased and demolished to provide a site, and an artificial mound created to give the building the prominence it merited. Civic projects are often fraught with problems of costs exceeding budgets and the conflict between quality and economy. An intense cause of discussion at Leeds was the tower, now a symbol of the city itself. Brodrick's original design for a tower had been rejected but it was agreed to make the foundations strong enough to carry one, and, when the work was half completed, the go-ahead was finally given.

Although Victorians are criticised for taking life too seriously, they celebrated public events with an enthusiasm surpassing anything which happens today. The processions, the banqueting, the orgy of oratory and the fireworks which marked the laying of the foundation stone in 1853 were totally eclipsed by the opening by Queen Victoria in 1858. Accounts of the euphoria engulfing Leeds are a joy to read. The welcoming party at the station provided another link with Hull: among the dignitaries was M. T. Baines, M.P. for Leeds and previously for Hull, and Viscount Goderich, M.P. for the West Riding, who had been elected for Hull in 1852 but unseated for illegal practices.

Some of the joy may have verged on hysteria, but Leeds had something to celebrate. The Victoria Hall is staggering in the exuberance of its design and the richness of its decoration, lavishly ornamented, and given a typically Victorian moral touch by such improving mottoes as, 'Weave Truth With Trust', and by a host of symbolic figures. At the entrance the commerce and industry of Leeds are portrayed giving encouragement to the arts and sciences — a theme relevant to modern ideas of industrial sponsorship. The grand frontage with its 'proud tower' dominates the streets below with awareness of its own superiority.

Brodrick's tussles with the builder formed a saga of frustration, and the massive restoration project which began in 1970 uncovered much inferior workmanship. With the aid of the British Museum the original

The Royal Institution, Albion Street, Hull, opened 1854, destroyed 1943.

colour scheme was identified and the Hall re-opened in all its glory in 1978.

In 1858 Brodrick moved to Leeds, and it was there that he created his next masterpiece, the Corn Exchange (1861), an elliptical domed building with a dramatic interior, the whole concept so brilliant that for once the word 'genius' is justified.

Hull, however, claimed his services again when, probably inspired by Leeds, the Corporation decided to have a purpose-built town hall instead of the 'temporary' premises they had been using since 1805, Alderman William Jarratt's house in Lowgate. Again there was the familiar routine, the ceremonial laying of the foundation stone in 1862, and the grand opening in 1866. Again, too, Viscount Goderich was there, though now transformed into Earl de Grey and Ripon, High Steward of Hull.

It was a fine building, but even Hull people would have to concede, not as overwhelming as Leeds Town Hall and on a far less prominent site, though a biased local historian claimed that it was 'not surpassed, if even it is equalled, in Great Britain'.

Cuthbert Brodrick had built the Leeds Mechanics Institute in 1865, and another heroic design was realised in 1867 at Scarborough with the building of the Grand Hotel, which Nikolaus Pevsner has described as a 'High Victorian gesture of assertion and confidence'. Some of his buildings were, of course, more modest, and some no longer exist. In Hull the Christ Church School (1849) which survived the blitz stands in a sorry state in Kingston Square, the sole survivor of his buildings in his native town apart from some minor work in a cemetery.

Leeds Town Hall was his greatest achievement, the pinnacle of his career. The rest of the story is sad and strange. He failed to make an impact outside Yorkshire and in 1869, when he was only 47, he abandoned architecture and left England for France. His meteoric career was finished. In 1899 he went to live with his niece in Jersey and died there in 1905.

The story also has an ironic footnote. Before many years had passed the Town Hall erected with such pride in Victorian Hull had become inadequate; an extension was started, but in 1912 Brodrick's building was demolished. The cupola has been placed in Pearson Park, and in 1918, when Victorian optimism had long evaporated, pieces of the old building were incorporated into a war memorial in the village of Brantingham.

Rose Carr
(1843-1913)
The Superwoman Carrier of Hornsea

Not everyone would agree with my admiration for Rose. But beneath the rough exterior which made Hornsea's hoi polloi *turn up their noses there was, in my opinion, a person — male or female — who deserves respect and admiration.*

Rose Carr is a name that carries a lot of weight with Holderness people — quite literally, too, for she weighed over 19 stone and had huge arms ending in hands of super-human grasp and grip.

And there lies the mystery of Rose Carr which will always be intriguing because it can never be solved: was Rose male or female?

She was certainly regarded as a girl when she was born in 1843 in North Frodingham, the daughter of John Carr, labourer and grocer, and his wife, Mary. Officially she was Rosamond Ellen, but the parson who baptised her wrote in the parish register 'Rosey Ellen'. After what must have been a very basic education, because she remained illiterate, Rose went into service at Dringhoe. Census records show that a teenage *John* Carr was working for a farmer there in 1861, possibly circumstantial evidence for the local tradition that Rose originally dressed like a boy and only took to female clothes in later years. At that time young boys wore frocks and had long hair and the genders were easier to fudge.

At some point Rose was kicked by a horse or a cow and the left side of her face was permanently paralysed, a disfigurement which made her a fearsome sight to most children. Mothers would try to quell unruly offspring by threatening to send for Rose Carr if they would not behave.

Rose had a rip-roaring reputation in the first part of her life, drinking heavily and ever-ready to start a fight, for she knew she would win. Then came a miraculous conversion. Like St. Paul on the road to Damascus, Rose saw the light in Beeford, renounced sin and became a doughty if unconventional Primitive Methodist.

She also moved to Hornsea and established a prosperous business as a carrier and coach proprietor. Rose may not have been the easiest of human companions but she had an innate understanding of horses. 'She loved horses and horses loved her,' was one man's verdict, and owners having problems with their animals would call on Rose for advice. Twice a week she made the long, slow journey to Hull, stopping at the Blue Bell, Ellerby, for her 'medicine'. Conversion had not lessened her liking for a large tot of whisky, and at the age of 29 she was still wild enough to be fined for reckless driving: it was not her first offence.

Rose also provided the equivalent of a taxi service in Hornsea, driving doctors and clergymen on their professional rounds, and she would race a rival to be first at the station to meet an incoming train. An astute business woman, she took advantage of her visits to Hull market to do a little horse-dealing. A favourite ploy was to sell a horse that was less manageable than she pretended and then buy it back cheaply from the distraught purchaser.

It would be hard to imagine a more unlikely preacher than Rose but, never satisfied with a passive role, she took her religion seriously and saw it as her duty to share her faith. She was never an eloquent speaker, charming a congregation with persuasive arguments and mellifluous phrases. Her style was rough and ready, but its simplicity and sincerity compensated for a lack of sophistication.

She relied on divine inspiration. Once, when the lamps were lit in Brandesburton Chapel as she was about to begin speaking, her theme presented itself with miraculous clarity. 'I didn't know what I was going

The best-known photograph of Rose Carr.

to preach about,' she said, 'but I do now — the light of the world.' There was nothing namby-pamby about her religion: the lesson she stressed was that good conduct receives its just reward. 'Noo, me lads and lasses,' she told one Holderness congregation, 'behave yersen so you will go to heaven. Then you'll get yersen an urn — not a penny urn, but a big un!'

Holderness people, however, remember Rose's amazing strength rather than her preaching. Her feats have become part of local folk-lore — how she hitched an 18-gallon barrel of beer on to a waggon; how she calmly picked up a 10-stone sack of corn under each arm and marched up the granary steps; and how she similarly carried two large rolls of linoleum from house to cart. Anyone foolhardy enough to insult her got more than they bargained for. To be flung head first out of a building by Rose or to have one's head banged against another's was no laughing matter. A discourteous Hull City footballer training in Hornsea received a ferocious ducking in a horse trough that took away his words and almost his life. Even more horrifying was the treatment handed out to a soldier who insulted her. Rose pretended to forgive him and held out her hand for a friendly shake. Rose took the soldier's hands and crushed them both in her own so hard that she broke his bones.

Medical men still discuss the phenomenon of Rose. Possibly she suffered from a rare condition; more probably there was some ambiguity in her make-up. Her voice was deep and gruff and there was a persistent rumour that she had fathered a son. Efforts to discover the truth by a bodily examination when she died in 1913 were frustrated by her sister, who speedily sewed her into her shroud, eternally safe from prying eyes.

Rose was feared by some and regarded with a wary respect by many, though there were others, more refined, who found her too vulgar for their taste. After a difficult life which she confronted by what was probably the only course open to her — ignoring public opinion and just being herself — she now lies at peace in Hornsea churchyard. The date of her death is wrongly given on her gravestone as '1912' and her age is recorded as '70', though she was in fact 69.

In recent years Rose has enjoyed a revival of posthumous fame. Those forced to live in a drabber, more conformist, world find her story exhilarating, and Dr. Stuart Walker has amassed a collection of anecdotes and material about Rose, now a star attraction in the North Holderness Museum of Village Life in Hornsea.

Her story is full of humour, but those of us interested in Rose have no desire to turn her into a mere figure of fun. Whatever her faults and whatever her gender, she was a remarkable human being and her life has its lessons for those more educated and sophisticated, and, not least, those who regard themselves as more 'normal'.

John Edward Champney and William Spencer
(1846-1929)   (1826-1910)
Creators of the Beverley Library

I spend a large part of my life in the Beverley Library and I have special reason for gratitude to the two men who brought it into existence: Champney, a Beverlonian in exile who always felt great loyalty to his home town, and Spencer, who was not Beverley born but developed great affection for the place where he had chosen to live and work.

John Edward Champney and William Spencer were both created honorary freemen of Beverley on the same day in 1906 but they had achieved that distinction by very different routes. When Champney was a young man he left Beverley, the town where he had been born, whereas Spencer only arrived in Beverley when he was 22 but remained there for the rest of his long life. Their careers and their fortunes had few similarities, but one thing they shared, a deep love of Beverley, and both names should be linked and honoured by all who use the Beverley Library.

Though Champney was the younger of the two, born on 31 May, 1846, he comes first in the story. His father, Thomas Frederick Champney, a newcomer to the town, was a solicitor who later took an active part in Beverley's rumbustious parliamentary elections; a few years ago, when his former offices, the building at the corner of Newbegin and Lairgate, were being cleared, an old annotated Beverley poll book was found lurking in one of the cupboards.

Before marriage Mrs. T. F. Champney was a Miss Ackroyd, a familiar surname in the West Riding, and it was in Halifax that young John Edward established himself as a prosperous businessman in the textile industry. He married Miss Margaret Huish but had no children and, as he grew older, his thoughts turned to helping his home town. Eventually he decided that the most effective way would be providing it with a much-needed library and museum. The offer was made in 1904, gratefully accepted by the Corporation, and on 8 August, 1906, he formally opened the building: when completed it was less than half its present size and consisted of the entrance hall, lending library and upstairs gallery.

J. E. Champney. *William Spencer.*

This is the point where Spencer's career converges with Champney's. Born in Rawcliffe in 1826, he had attended Drax Grammar School before becoming a student at the Glasgow Free Church Training College. After an 18-month stint in his first post at Sowerby Bridge he was appointed headmaster of the Wesleyan Day School, Beverley, in 1848.

Spencer was no transient passenger, more intent on self-advancement than attention to the children in his charge; he remained at the school for 39 years, a man of profound influence on the estimated 4,000 pupils for whom he was responsible over that long period and certainly one deserving the description which has since become a glibly-used cliché — 'a dedicated teacher'. As the ultimate recognition of his 'long and honourable career', the school was renamed in 1894 the Spencer Council School.

The conclusion of his teaching career gave him the opportunity for another form of public service. In 1888 he was elected to the Council, was elevated to the status of alderman in 1895, and in 1904 became mayor in a ceremony which had particular significance for him because he was invested with the insignia of office by one of his old boys, Alderman Harry Wray. This was a time when members of local councils spoke and acted more on individual judgment and toed the party line less than they do today. So much so that it was often difficult to determine where Spencer's political sympathies lay; when questioned, he would always answer that he was not a party man. Although Nonconformists generally became closely identified with the Liberal Party, there was a tendency for many Wesleyans to vote Conservative, and in his later period Spencer seemed to be leaning more towards the Tories.

Spencer was elected mayor for a second term in 1905 and he was, therefore, in office when the Library was under discussion. A condition of Champney's gift was that the Corporation should provide a suitable site and it was this which gave Spencer his own opportunity of helping his fellow Beverlonians. Although he had little inclination for playing the role of a free-spending mayor and hosting grand social functions which would earn him easy but meaningless popularity, he was a generous-hearted man. The site on which the Library was being built was mortgaged. Spencer saw this as a burden on the ratepayers and he put his money to use in a most practical way by giving the considerable sum of £520 4s. and paying off the debt.

The opening ceremony in 1906, followed by the conferment of honorary freedoms on Champney and Spencer, and by a luncheon in the mayor's parlour, was the sort of event in which Beverley's Edwardian civic leaders revelled, indulging in a feast of oratory and a plethora of elegantly-worded compliments to each other. Alderman James Elwell (the woodcarver), Chairman of the Library Committee, presented Champney with 'a gold key of very artistic design' to open the new building and then retain as a memento, while Dr. Mitchell Wilson, President of the grand-sounding Beverley Literary and Scientific Society, presented Champney with an address. In return the town received a portrait of Champney and a tall-case clock in the Chippendale style.

Now exiled in plush Hans Place (near Harrods), and with a country house in Buckinghamshire, Champney was in nostalgic mood and 'looked back with feelings of affection to those days when he could go and roam over the Westwood'. Many tributes were paid to Spencer, who responded with equal eloquence. He would rather, he said, be a freeman of Beverley than of ancient Rome: the town had given him every honour it could bestow.

He died at his home in Railway Street on 25 February, 1910, at the age of 83 and in his will left a further magnificent gift of £5,000 to the Library and Museum. Not so grand, but a delightful gesture, was his legacy of £100 to provide each child at his old school with a yearly gift of an orange, a fruit then regarded as quite a treat and often encountered only in the foot of a Christmas stocking. The first distribution was in 1911 and, although the money has long run out, the custom is still maintained in an updated form with an orange, donated by the Israeli Citrus Board, presented to each child at Swinemoor Junior School, the successor to the old Spencer Council School.

The original donation was not the end of Champney's munificence. Later he decided to leave money for extending the Library, but in the event he put the plan into operation in his life-time. Accordingly a wing was added which included the reference library and the extension to the art gallery above, although he was too ill to attend the official opening in December, 1928. This time he also provided the land and paid £1,250 for the laying out of a garden to the rear and side. Even so, on his death in 1929 he left a further £5,000 to establish a trust fund for the reference library, £1,600 to create the Champney Garden Endowment Fund, and his own fine collection of over 5,000 volumes to the Library, including some rare and beautiful items, now of great value.

One sad footnote to the story concerned his bequest for a stained glass window in Beverley Minster to commemorate himself and his wife. The vicar, Dr. W. H. Rigg, proved most unco-operative and Champney's solicitor complained of the 'very rude treatment we have received' and his 'extraordinary way of behaving', not least his initial offensive rejection of the distinguished artist's drawing with the curt note: 'The design you have sent me will not do.'

After much tricky negotiating he finally came round, and the attractive window was installed in the south wall of the great south transept. But stained glass windows and honorary freedoms are nothing compared to the greatest tribute Champney and Spencer could ever be paid — the pleasure, interest and usefulness the Library has given to thousands of readers over the years.

Madame Clapham
(Mrs. Emily Clapham)
(1856-1952)
Society Dressmaker

Everyone seems to enjoy hearing about Madame Clapham, one of those many characters who are easier to cope with as historical figures than they were by those who had to work with them. I would love to know more about her husband, Haigh. Did she treat him as badly as she did her other subordinates?

Hull as a centre of fashion sounds a bizarre idea. Yet, at the turn of the century, ladies with titles — and wealthy husbands to foot the bill — came to Hull for the dresses which would draw admiring glances as they moved gracefully among the privileged ranks of high society.

The magnet which attracted them to Hull was a dressmaker in Kingston Square who styled herself Madame Clapham and described her profession as costumier. As a boy, the author Sir Osbert Sitwell remembered travelling by train from Scarborough with his mother, the vivacious Lady Ida, and her cousin Lady Westmorland, to be fitted for a court ball. 'Hull,' he writes, 'was the rage.'

Madame Clapham, who began life as Emily McVitie in Cheltenham in 1856, had herself made the journey from Scarborough (where she had served an apprenticeship with Marshall & Snelgrove), when she and her husband, Haigh Clapham, had decided to set up business in Hull in 1887. It was an inspired choice. Hull was an expanding town with a flourishing trade, and ten years later was to be designated a city. There were wealthy people who had benefited from this prosperity and lived in fine houses in the town or, increasingly, in the pleasant villages to the west, the type of affluent customer on whom the ambitious Mrs. Clapham had set her eyes.

And Kingston Square was what the Victorians called 'a good address,' in the heart of a 'respectable' residential area with large houses and impressive public buildings. It was part of Hull's Georgian suburbs, developed in the period following the opening of the first dock in 1778. The mediaeval walls were demolished, Hull was able to spread into rural Sculcoates, and smart streets of elegant houses were built: Albion Street, Baker Street, Pryme Street, Story Street and Wright Street.

Madame Clapham.

(Peter Walker)

Kingston Square itself had been developed at the beginning of the 19th century by the Reverend Robert Jarratt: a splendid example of Georgian town planning with a central garden to which the residents of the surrounding houses had their keys. In one corner was the Anglican Christ Church, opened in 1822, for the convenience of worshippers who had moved out to the Old Town: the parents of 'Lewis Carroll' (Charles Lutwidge Dodgson) were married there in 1827, for the Lutwidge home was at 7 Charlotte Street.

Not far away, at the corner of Jarratt Street, the Assembly Rooms (1834) were the focal point of Victorian and Edwardian social life, the scene of splendid banquets, concerts and functions attended by the upper échelons of Hull and the East Riding. The Assembly Rooms were the expected venue for addresses by distinguished visiting speakers and it was there that Charles Dickens mesmerised audiences with his dramatic readings from his novels.

Across Jarratt Street was the Renaissance-style Clowes Chapel (1851), the near neighbour of Hull's greatest post-Reformation Catholic Church, St. Charles, opened in 1829, the year of Emancipation, and still one of this area's lesser-known splendours. 'The calm exterior,' one writer has pointed out, 'gives no hint of the Baroque drama inside.' Facing the Assembly Rooms across the garden was the classical façade of the Hull and East Riding School of Medicine and Anatomy, which enabled students to complete their medical training in Hull until 1869, after which it became the Blind Institute.

Haigh and Emily Clapham had originally invested their entire savings in a Victorian house, Number 1, Kingston Square, but by the end of the century they had acquired No. 2, and by 1912 No. 3, an impressive range of property and an indication of the growth of the business. Although Madame Clapham retained a bedroom at No. 3, the main residence from the late 19th Century was a beautiful house in South Street, Cottingham. Haigh, a shadowy figure, plays only a supporting role in the story of success.

Madame Clapham's meteoric rise would not have happened without the patronage of the Wilson girls, the daughters of the shipping magnates, Arthur Wilson of Tranby Croft and his brother Charles Henry (later Lord Nunburnholme) of Warter Priory. The Wilson family entered London society and the ladies, particularly Muriel, Arthur's beautiful daughter, were so envied for their stylish gowns that they set a fashion that others longed to follow. Madame Clapham thought advertising vulgar and relied on her customers' recommendations!

A journalist writing in *The Hull Lady,* a glossy magazine, in 1901, wrote a delightfully obsequious account of her visit to Madame Clapham. She was in ecstacy as Madame escorted her through the hall into a large and spacious room, beautifully carpeted with a deep rich

Haigh Clapham.

A Madame Clapham creation specially made for a great occasion. The lady was Mrs. Fanny Riley (née Wallace) who was attending the opening of a dock in Swansea.

Kingston Theatre Hotel, former premises of Madame Clapham.

crimson pile, the walls of pink artistically draped with linen tissue. This was the showroom, an Aladdin's Cave of beautiful, expensive things, and the description rose in a crescendo of praise: 'I particularly noticed a French model gown in black velvet, handsomely embroidered with *écru* lace *appliqué,* and a princess robe in blue Orient satin, charmingly trimmed with blue *mousseline de soie;* there were also several lovely evening cloaks about, one, which specially took my attention, being in banana coloured cloth with a beautiful, old muslin collar and necklet of ermine.'

Madame Clapham's most prestigious client, from whom she earned the right to style herself 'Court Dressmaker', was Queen Maud of Norway, the daughter of Edward VII, who did not visit Kingston Square but stayed at Appleton House, Sandringham, or Claridges, where Madame Clapham took a selection of dresses for her consideration. One story handed down is that, on the first visit, Queen Maud spoke so quietly that Madame Clapham, who was deaf but did not wear a hearing aid, had to have the royal words interpreted by a mannequin.

Stories of Madame Clapham abound, for she had at her peak 150 employees. Some ex-Clapham seamstresses are still alive, and others have left behind ancedotes which now form a fascinating store of oral history. Miss Enid Paterson of Cottingham told me something which has not, I think, appeared in print before: her mother, then Miss Alice Rounding, who worked for Madame Clapham, had the same measurements as Queen Maud and acted as the living model for the royal dresses.

Madame Clapham was a dominating — and domineering — figure with a high regard for high social status. Only the favoured received her personal attention. The dresses were expensive but money was not a thing a lady discussed. Such talk was as vulgar as the advertising Madame despised and it was customary to forward the bill discreetly to a husband so that the lady's eyes would not be offended by anything as unfeminine as an invoice.

In her interview with *The Hull Lady,* Madame Clapham spoke of her plans for expansion: 'I am having the showrooms enlarged and extensive alterations made during the next three months, also more work-rooms added ... I must have more room.' Her employees saw the less glamorous side of the business, working in bare rooms which were bitterly cold in winter. A girl who had an aptitude for a particular task would be kept at it for years doing nothing else. Madame ruled over her kingdom like an unbenevolent dictator. Her temper was legendary and she was known to tear a garment to pieces if it did not satisfy her scrutiny. She was equally despotic with her domestic staff in Cottingham.

When part of the Clapham premises, Nos. 1 and 2, were converted into the Kingston Theatre Hotel in 1987, Mrs. Gladys Carmichael, who had started work there as a seamstress in 1916, was guest of honour at the official opening of the hotel. She had been paid 3s. 6d a week and spent most of her time on her hands and knees picking up pins.

In contrast to the seductive atmosphere of the showroom which entranced *The Hull Lady,* the workrooms had no carpets, no comfortable furniture, only bare boards. Factory laws regulating the hours worked by young girls were ignored, and Mrs. Carmichael recalled: 'I remember myself and other juniors hidden in small, dark cupboards so the inspectors did not see that we were having to work into the evening.'

The First World War marked the end of an era with a finality rare in history. Fashions and social attitudes changed, and the Bright Young Things of the Twenties no longer wanted dresses in the styles which Madame Clapham had supplied for the ladies of a less hectic period. Her golden age had been the last years of Victoria and the 'long Edwardian summer' which followed. The business, however, continued, a pale reflection of the great days of international success, even through the Second World War and into the postwar world. Madame Clapham died in 1952 aged 96. Numbers 1 and 2 were sold but Miss Emily Wall, her niece, carried on at No. 3 until 1967.

In history the themes of change and continuity are rarely far apart. There are clear and welcome indications that the slow decline of Kingston Square, which became rather shabby, is now over. The houses are smarter and the New Theatre (converted from the Assembly Rooms in 1939 and still retaining the original Ionic columns at the front and side) has been substantially improved and is attracting better shows and bigger audiences so that, on a good evening, the Square is once again a lively place to be.

The central garden has been redesigned and is now open to all, and above the entrance to the Kingston Theatre Hotel, the former premises of the 'Court Dressmaker', the name 'Claphams' has been placed as an appropriate reminder of Kingston Square's most famous resident.

Rev. Joseph Coltman
(1775-1837)
Clergyman and Public Benefactor

It is impossible to leave Joseph Coltman out of this book. Most people have heard of him, but for the wrong reasons. He deserves being remembered as more than a comic character.

History has not been kind to Joseph Coltman. He is remembered as a comic figure, absurdly fat — at 37 stones the heaviest man in England. All this is irrelevant. Beneath the gross exterior was a kind and cultured gentleman.

His own background was privileged. The Coltmans were an upper-class landowning family and Joseph, born in 1775, was at Charterhouse School and Trinity College, Cambridge, before being ordained as an Anglican clergyman.

In 1806 he came to Beverley as assistant curate at the Minster, and when the vicar died seven years later he was appointed to the senior post. For a time he lived at Amphion House, just outside North Bar, but then moved into his official residence — now the Old Vicarage — which needed certain strengthening and widening before it could cope with an occupant of his dimensions. One reference book mentions a wife, but the evidence indicates that he remained a bachelor. Many now know of Joseph Coltman through the silhouette depicting him and his velocipede, or dandy-horse, an early type of two-wheeler, which supported him, with a rope attached and pulled along by a boy, as he moved around his parish. Contemporaries recall how it travelled with him in his carriage, how his footman rode it outside the Vicarage to amuse spectators, how he once toppled over into the ditch in the part of Well Lane which is now Champney Road, and how he was propelled up a ramp into his pulpit by three vergers.

These anecdotes make history fun, but they completely distort the reputation of a man of character and achievement. Coltman was a scholar who wrote the history of the Minster and 'never seemed so happily employed as when he was instructing young men'. Before breakfast he would go to the Grammar School and help the boys with their Greek and Latin, and for his devotion to the Blue Coat School he was granted the freedom of Beverley in 1810.

The famous silhouette of Coltman with his dandy horse.

Rev. Joseph Coltman.

Coltman Street, Hull, undergoing restoration.

In an age when antagonism between rival religious groups was often bitter, Joseph Coltman distinguished himself by rising above such petty and degrading sectarian squabbles. The proposal to grant Catholics equal civil rights with Protestants in 1829 was far too advanced for some, like the Mayor of Beverley, who summoned a meeting of leading residents at the Guildhall to organise a petition of protest against such an outrageous notion. Coltman attended and spoke out fearlessly. He did not believe that the meeting reflected the feeling of the town: 'He should wish to leave it to the sense of Parliament.'

He died in appallingly cruel circumstances in 1837, turning over in bed and suffocating with his face in the pillow when his weight made it impossible for him to right himself. Humiliatingly, too, he was lowered into his grave with a block and tackle used for lifting masonry at the Minster, and it was ironic that his funeral should have been conducted by his assistant curate, William Hildyard, a narrow-minded, rather unpleasant man who had not been the most supportive of colleagues. It is agreeable to think of Hildyard being obliged to say nice things about Joseph before the Minster congregation. Did he, one wonders, damn him with faint praise?

The following day a glowing tribute was paid to his talents and virtues and he was praised as an eloquent and faithful pastor of great learning, integrity and benevolence, proverbially kind to the poor, a friend and adviser to the widow and the orphan, a father to the fatherless, and a man of unfailing common sense and kindness, who could mix as easily with humbler people as he could with men of rank and education.

A superb memorial in the north aisle of the nave of the Minster is a permanent tribute to his outstanding attainments and there are other reminders of the Coltmans in Hull. The family owned land which was ripe for development at a time when the town was experiencing a massive increase in population and decided that it would be more profitable to turn fields into streets. Coltman Street had the finest residences and proudly bore the family name. Bacheler Street honours a family into which the Coltmans had married, and King's Bench Street and Queensgate Street were named after Coltman addresses in London.

Local people probably smiled knowingly when they read one sentence in Joseph Coltman's obituary: 'Of a truth it may be said that a great man has fallen in Beverley.'

The greatness was more in his character than in his avoirdupois.

Sir Thomas Aston Clifford Constable
(1807-1870)
A Young Man of Privilege

Sir Thomas Aston Clifford Constable only just qualifies for this collection. A rather grey figure when he was a young parliamentary candidate, he derived his position from birth, not outstanding ability or impressive personality. But inherited wealth and status enabled a colourless candidate to make a colourful impact on the community.

A colourful cavalcade makes a glittering spectacle as it moves in stately progress along the country roads of Holderness.

The leading vehicle, a landau, is followed by a barouche and pair. Then comes a vast number of open carriages and, finally, riders, three abreast. Windows, chimneys and tops of houses along the route are decorated with crimson and yellow flags, and spectators on both sides of the roads wave flags or sport ribbons of the same colours. By the time the whole procession has formed, a mile separates the leading landau from the riders at the rear.

This is no fantasy but an accurate description of the scene on 30 July, 1830, when Sir Thomas Aston Clifford Constable drove in style from his stately home, Burton Constable, to be elected M.P. for Hedon. It was a historic event in every way. Constable had only just become eligible to stand for Parliament. He was a member of a Catholic family and, although Constables had been M.P.s for Hedon in the 16th and 17th centuries, their religion had thereafter barred them from the Commons until the Catholic Emancipation Act of 1829.

The Borough of Hedon was an obvious constituency for the Constables. They were the great landed family of the area, wielding enormous influence and enjoying considerable wealth — an essential qualification for anyone who aspired to represent Hedon in Parliament. Hedon had a long tradition of bribery and corruption, and the fortunate minority with a vote — just over 300 men — expected something tangible from the candidate they supported: not merely political promises but money payments as well as copious supplies of free food and drink in the inns with which Hedon was well supplied.

Such a tiny electorate meant that each voter could be personally nobbled, an activity at which Hedon's most formidable political figure,

*James Iveson, 1770-1850,
Town Clerk of Hedon for over 40 years.*

Sir Thomas Aston Clifford Constable.

Hedon Town Hall in the 19th century.

the long-serving Town Clerk, James Iveson, was adept. Though he never attempted to enter Parliament himself, he was the man who pulled the strings for the candidates he supported; very quickly they discovered that *they* were the ones dancing to *his* tune. James, like his father and brother (both William), was a lawyer. There was a close professional relationship between the Ivesons and the Constables, and the stage was set for Sir Thomas to enter into the inheritance from which his religion had until recently excluded him.

Apart from his social position and wealth he had few of the attributes expected of a man about to embark on a public career. He was only 23 and Richard Bethell, M.P., of Rise Park, a neighbouring landowner, described him unenthusiastically as 'a young man not much accustomed to public life', though he argued that 'he was now called upon to fill a situation to which his rank and station in the country entitled him'.

For a reserved young gentleman a boisterous early 19th-century election must have presented a frightening contrast to the privileged life-style within the confines of Burton Constable park and, though the people cheered as the brilliant procession made its magnificent progress past the fields and farms which were largely his, for he owned over 12,000 Holderness acres, this was a day when he might well have preferred obscurity to the ordeal awaiting him in Hedon.

He was a last-minute candidate. A major obstacle to his standing was that Hedon already had two well-established M.P.s, Robert Farrand and Colonel John Baillie, and there seemed every prospect that they would offer themselves for re-election.

Baillie, however (who had probably had his fill of Hedon politics), made a surprise announcement that he was standing at Inverness, where he was a landed proprietor, and the way was clear for Constable to fill the vacancy. First, he was obliged to submit to a traditional piece of Hedon blackmail by paying the substantial sum of 200 guineas into the town coffers in order to be enrolled as a freeman — a formality it was unwise to neglect, although there was no legal obligation for a candidate to have freeman status.

In his election address Constable explained his late appearance, and also revealed that he already possessed something of the astuteness of a practised politician. As a Catholic he had been unable to attend university and, instead, travelled abroad: anticipating snide chauvinistic comments about his ignorance of English life and politics, he claimed that his period on the Continent 'only served to produce in him a higher regard for the blessings we here enjoy under our glorious constitution'.

And so, early in the morning, after an 'elegant and seasonal refreshment' in the great hall of his residence, the young baronet and his wife were escorted to their landau and, followed by a loyal retinue, passed through the park and out into the country lanes beyond, the

Burton Constable Hall.

procession reinforced by more riders and carriages as it travelled through Sproatley and into Preston, where the last riders brought up the rear as Sir Thomas's landau reached the Hedon boundary. Another carefully staged ritual was then performed. Constable supporters removed the four horses from his vehicle and, preceded by a strategically placed band, pulled it triumphantly into Hedon.

After this stupendous build-up, the election itself was bound to be an anti-climax. There was no hint of anxiety about the result for Hedon was represented by two M.P.s and there were only two candidates, a terrible disappointment to voters deprived of the customary competitive bribery by candidates bidding for votes. As a feeble substitute, and to inject a little excitement into the proceedings, some even suggested having a (totally unnecessary) poll to determine Constable and Farrand's order of popularity, but nothing came of the absurd notion.

Overwhelmed by the noise and commotion, and no doubt anxious about what might happen to him, the timid young aristocrat is said to have shaken like a leaf at his nomination. He survived, only to undergo the doubtful and sometimes dangerous honour of being 'chaired', that is placed in a ceremonial chair and carried shoulder-high, to give the people of Hedon an opportunity of gazing in admiration at their new M.P. — or hurling insults or unpleasant objects at him. A dinner followed at the King's Head, and 'open house' was kept at other inns where everyone consumed as much free drink as possible on the understanding that the cost (often grossly inflated by the publican) would be borne by the successful candidates.

Constable's parliamentary career was brief and his impact on national events nil. This was the time of fierce controversy over the Reform Bill. A year later, in 1831, Parliament was dissolved and another general election followed in which he and Farrand were re-elected, again without a contest. In 1832 the Bill became an Act and Hedon, notorious as a rotten borough, with no logical case for separate representation in Parliament when such growing towns as Sheffield had no such right, was an obvious casualty and lost its two M.P.s. Two new roads, Constable Garth and Farrand Road, now commemorate this lively period in the town's history.

Sir Thomas lived until 1870 but, deprived of the seat which he had so recently become entitled to occupy, made no attempt to represent any other constituency. Most probably he had decided that enough was enough.

The sensible people are those who know when to call it a day.

William Constable
(c.1794 or c.1800*-1867)
Shoemaker and Practical Joker

I imagine I should have avoided Billy Constable like the plague if I had known him, but, at a safe distance, transformed into a minor character with a walk-on part in the history of Beverley, he sounds quite funny.

Beverley's Guildhall has become more accessible with regular open days. Even so, a close watch is kept on its treasures and it would be rather difficult for a visitor to remove any of its contents.

But in the early 19th century one man — incredibly — walked out with the mace. The incident was described in *The Express* (27 October, 1883), a local newspaper then running a series of reminiscences by an old but anonymous freeman.

He had clear memories of the miscreant: a cobbler named Billy Constable but known to his cronies as 'Napoleon Bonaparte', whom he somehow resembled. Billy was even better known for his fondness for drink and, once he had settled in the chimney corner of an inn, he stayed there until his money ran out.

Under the influence of drink he turned into an early version of Jeremy Beadle, dreaded by landlords who suffered from his practical jokes. Favourite tricks were flavouring the publican's tea by popping a lump of tobacco into the kettle boiling on the inn fire or mixing gunpowder with the sawdust of a spittoon and waiting merrily for warm ash from a pipe to cause the inevitable explosion.

Billy was familiar with the inside of the Guildhall and was accustomed to being hauled up before the Bench on a Monday morning after Saturday night's over-indulgence. When Alderman Marmaduke Hewitt was mayor and chief magistrate in 1821-2 (not 1810 as the old freeman thought), he had given Billy one last chance: 'Six shillings costs, and if you are brought here again I shall order you to be placed in the stocks.'

---

*Two shoemakers named William Constable died in Beverley in 1867. One, aged 73, from Butcher Row died of inflamation of the back. The youngest one, aged 67, from Lairgate, died of apoplexy.

Magistrates' Room, Guildhall, Beverley.

Green Dragon, Beverley.

Marmaduke Hewitt, the mayor on whom William Constable took his revenge.

1820-1   S. HALL.
1821-2   M. HEWITT.
1822-3   T. HULL.

Those words rankled, but revenge came one glorious summer's day. The sun shone down on empty streets, the only signs of life a few dogs sprawling in shop doorways, the only sounds the shouts of a coalman walking alongside his cart, and 'the lazy rumble of an empty wagon' on its homeward journey from Beckside where it had delivered its load of corn.

Into this idyllic scene stepped — or rather staggered — Billy, somewhat muddled after a lengthy session at his favourite pub, the Green Dragon. He followed a zig-zag route along the street, kicking the occasional dog on his way, and ending up near the Guildhall. The door was open, no one was about, and Billy saw the perfect opportunity for revenging himself on Mayor Hewitt. With difficulty he negotiated the doorway, the passage and the staircase. On the table in the upper room (the Magistrates' Room then used for Council meetings) was the mace, ready for the mace bearer and civic officials to attend at the mayor's house and escort him in state to the meeting, a delightful ceremony sadly no longer practicable.

Billy picked up the mace, walked out into the deserted street and dropped it in an open section of the old Walker Beck, where it lay camouflaged by mud and sewage for three months.

When the loss was discovered Beverley was in a state of shock, and more than half a century later the old freeman remembered the furore. Rewards were offered but the mystery remained unsolved.

Fate then intervened. Billy's alcoholic habits were sapping his health; he took to his bed, and began to worry about the eternal consequences of his crime, though the details were so confused that he wondered if it was all just a figment of his fevered imagination. Eventually he was in such distress that he begged his mother to go to Alderman Hewitt and reveal the resting place of the missing mace.

Nothing is worse than telling the truth and not being believed. Mrs. Constable had a hard struggle to be taken seriously but at last the spot identified by her son was searched and the mace found, no worse for wear. The account of Beverley's reaction to the news rings true. Some believed no punishment too severe, but most enjoyed every minute.

Billy did not die. Like many hypochondriacs, he grossly underestimated his bodily powers and had more than 40 years before him. His recovery, though, was prolonged and by the time he appeared in court official anger had subsided and he was merely given another last warning.

In the history of Beverley the episode is trivial, but unimportant events can bring the past to life as vividly as great occasions.

William Crosskill
(1800-1888)
Beverley's Pioneer of Engineering

Those who try but fail can be more attractive than the successful: most of us know more about failure than we do success. William Crosskill was a man of enormous ability and vision who had the misfortune to be born too early, before ways of financing his business became available for entrepreneurs like himself.

Crosskill House, the name of the new office block in Mill Lane opened by the Duchess of Kent, is a timely reminder of a man who played an important part in 19th-century Beverley.

William Crosskill was not quite a self-made man but he did not begin his career with exceptional advantages. His father, who ran a one-man business as a whitesmith, died in 1812, leaving a widow and seven children. The eldest, William, was only 12, but he and his mother carried on the business to maintain the family income, and even managed to expand it.

This was a time of thrusting entrepreneurs, and England was enjoying a golden age of inventive genius. It was a period made for the ambitious, youthful William and by 1825 he had built an iron foundry where he installed a steam engine. He was ready to turn his hand to anything, from hanging the Minster bells to manufacturing lamp posts: some bearing his name are still in use.

But it was as an agricultural engineer that he earned a reputation which spread far beyond Beverley. The population was expanding, thousands were emigrating to try their hand at opening up the hitherto unfarmed acres of the New World and Australasia. There was a need for better equipment and greater agricultural efficiency and it was a demand that William Crosskill was happy to meet. His iron works in Mill Lane began turning out ploughs, carts and a variety of implements, among them the most ingenious invention of all, the ugly-sounding but invaluable clod-crusher for use on heavy land. The clod-crusher was displayed at the Great Exhibition and Crosskill became Beverley's major employer. By 1853 a massive workforce of 800 men was employed on the seven-acre site in Mill Lane.

A business growing at such a phenomenal rate needed more capital than one man could provide from his private resources. Limited

William Crosskill.

companies with investment opportunities for the public were not authorised by Parliament until 1856, and Crosskill was dependent on a large bank loan from the East Riding Bank, with a mortgage on his property as security.

Even a thriving concern can fail through lack of liquidity — the familiar cash-flow problem — and it was a tragedy for William Crosskill that at the peak of his prosperity in 1855 the bank demanded the repayment of the loan. Whether the bankers were motivated by jealousy, the fear of having too many eggs in one basket, or some other factor, is unknown. Whatever the reason, Crosskill was unable to pay back the massive loan of over £70,000 and the bank assumed control of the business as trustees, though his sons, Alfred and Edmund, continued to manage it. William Crosskill himself retired to Walkergate House, a substantial residence, which bears a plaque commemorating its most famous occupant. He had been mayor in 1848 and his bust stands in the window recess of the Magistrates' Room at the Guildhall.

After a legal action in 1863 Alfred and Edmund withdrew from the firm and set up a new business, William Crosskill & Sons, in Eastgate. Alfred carried on alone after Edmund's death in 1891 and after his own death the business was taken over by the East Yorkshire Cart and Waggon Company Ltd.

A failure only by the narrowest legal criteria, William Crosskill deserves a place of honour as one of the minor celebrities of Victorian England, a man who made a major contribution to the economy of Beverley and to improved agriculture at home and abroad.

Edmund's grandson, W. E. (Ted) Crosskill, still lives in Sussex, and five years ago told the story of his Edwardian childhood in his book, *First Beginnings*. In spite of 'trouble at t'mill' the Crosskills remained one of Beverley's leading families and Ted Crosskill has happy memories of his early idyllic years at 72 Lairgate where his parents lived a comfortable life, served by a cook, housemaid, nanny and gardener.

His reminiscences, like the bust in the Guildhall and Crosskill House, maintain a link with a family important in the story of Beverley. If the bank had not foreclosed, if the business had evolved — like Reckitt's — into a great international company, how different the last century of Beverley's history might have been!

Walkergate House, now bearing Beverley and District Civic Society's plaque.

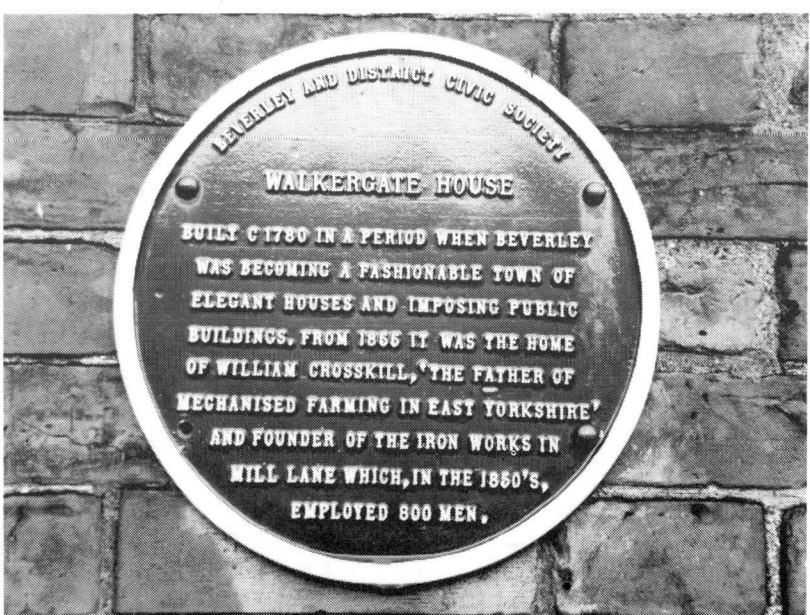

Thomas Robinson Ferens
(1847-1930)
Businessman and Benefactor

Ferens is one of those characters who led lives so filled with professional and public duties and inspired by such lofty ideals that most of us can only stand and stare in amazement. As a graduate of Hull University I owe a special debt to him. I find it difficult, though, to get beneath his skin and discover the man behind the public figure.

Ferensway escaped being named Quality Street only by the skin of its teeth.

The bizarre name, Quality Street, had been agreed in committee, but it was finally decided to use the opportunity to honour T. R. Ferens, who had recently died. It was one of those occasions when second thoughts are definitely best. Thomas Robinson Ferens was a not a local lad, but he had lived in Hull for over 60 years and it was there that he found his spiritual home. He was fiercely loyal to his adopted city and no benefactor has equalled his generosity.

Ferens was born in 1847 in New Shildon, County Durham, where his father owned a small mill; in old age he recalled the happy times spent swimming in the mill stream. He attended the Belvedere Academy, a private school in Bishop Auckland, but left when he was 13 to work in the office of the Stockton and Darlington Railway. Six years later he became a clerk with an engineering company, and in 1868 moved to Hull to take up the post of shorthand and confidential clerk to James Reckitt at an annual salary of £70. Those who remember Ferens recall how he always stressed the value of shorthand — as a young man he kept in practice on a Sunday by taking down the sermon in shorthand.

Isaac Reckitt, James' father, had arrived in Hull in 1840 and the family firm had had a rough ride in its early years. The discovery of soluble starch, however, put the Reckitts on the road that eventually led to massive expansion and international success, and the sternly moral style in which the business was managed provided the ideal environment for an ambitious, able and hard-working young man like Ferens to impress his employers.

By 1874 he had been promoted to Works Manager, and then he found his metier by transferring to the commercial and administrative side of the business, successively occupying the whole spectrum of senior appointments — as Secretary, General Manager, Director and Chairman. It was not exactly a story of rags to riches but it was a shining example of a man of high ability, but no influence or privilege, having

Thomas R. Ferens.

Holderness House.

his endeavours crowned with the success that virtue deserves but often fails to achieve. He was a trim, upright figure who expected the high standards from others that he imposed on himself; he set great store on a smart appearance and he was a stickler for punctuality, frequently in his office by 6 a.m. His memory for faces was said to be phenomenal.

The Reckitts had an enlightened attitude to their role as employers and provided welfare and educational facilities long before they became the norm in large companies. Their management style was based on their Quaker principles, while Ferens, also an exponent of the Protestant work ethic, was a committed Wesleyan, a worshipper at Brunswick Chapel on Holderness Road, devoted to its Sunday School (said to be the largest in Yorkshire), and a teacher there to the very end of his life.

He saw it as his duty to contribute to national affairs and, although defeated as a Liberal candidate in East Hull in 1900, he was successful in the Liberal landslide of 1906, and celebrated by giving each employee a sovereign which he asked should not be spent on intoxicating liquor. The *Hull Daily Mail* reported unsympathetically his performance at a meeting held at the Assembly Rooms (now the New Theatre) during that campaign: 'Enter Mr. Ferens, pallid, extempore and business-like. His voice is somewhat anxious and metallic. He appears hot and somewhat pained but gets his coat off with the air in which a sexton might encounter a highwayman.'

A late arrival at Westminster — almost 60 when he was first elected — Ferens was not a frequent speaker but was regarded with respect, and in 1912 became a Privy Councillor. He continued to represent East Hull until defeat in 1918.

He had married Esther Ellen Field, daughter of William Field, a Wesleyan merchant whose grocery business and associated café still arouse pleasant memories in Hull. It was a happy, though childless, marriage, and during parliamentary sessions Mr. and Mrs. Ferens returned from London each weekend to teach the Brunswick School children who were in some measure their surrogate family. At one period the Ferens lived at Saxby House, 346 Holderness Road, but their final home, where they moved in 1909, was the fine residence, Holderness House. In spite of considerable wealth they lived there in comfortable but in no way ostentatious style.

Ferens was an astute businessman, and a profit-sharing contract brought him a considerable income as Reckitt's grew ever more prosperous. His upbringing, his religion and his character all combined to ensure that he never saw money as a means of purchasing luxuries for himself but as a resource which it was his responsibility to channel into outlets where it would do most good.

A number of organisations outside the town received his financial

The Garden Village, opened 1908.
The foundation of Reckitt's.
Hull University: one of the two original buildings opened 1928.

(Mervyn Kirby)

support, but Hull was always the principal object of his charity, and his remarkable list of benefactions included the land for East Park boating lake, a recreation ground for the Y.P.I., the Ferens Art Gallery (with money to buy paintings), and, most important of all (for he was particularly anxious that a great city like Hull should have a university), the site and £¼ million endowment to establish the University College. Appropriately the University's motto is a Latin pun on his name: *Lampada Ferens* — 'carrying the lamp (of learning)'.

One scheme in which he was involved has given Hull a splendid piece of Edwardian town planning. In 1907 Sir James Reckitt put forward his ideas for improving the living conditions of their employees in a letter to Ferens: 'Whilst I and my family are living in beautiful houses, surrounded by lovely gardens and fine scenery, the workpeople we employ are, many of them, living in squalor, and all of them without gardens in narrow streets and alleys. It seems to me the time has come . . . to establish a Garden Village, within a reasonable distance of our works . . . I would not feel comfortable did I not give you and some others the opportunity of joining in, and getting some pleasure and satisfaction out of it.' The outcome was the opening of the Garden Village in 1908.

Ferens was typical of the Nonconformist outlook of that period in his hostility to alcohol, and the Garden Village had its club and institute but no public house. One local poet wrote some delightful verses which begin:

> 'O! Garden Village folk are proud
> As they have right to be,
> Whose houses stand but two by two,
> With every house a tree.'

They end on the same ironical note:

> 'I'd almost turn a Wesleyan
> To live like Garden Village folk.'

With increasing age Ferens' sight began to fail, and, though he continued to teach his Sunday School pupils, the time came when the class had to be held at Holderness House. He died on 9 May, 1930, after eight years of widowhood and both he and Mrs. Ferens were, as they wished, cremated and their ashes buried in their own garden. Holderness House itself was left as a home for gentlewomen.

Some of Ferens' ideas, attitudes and actions now seem dated, but, whatever his limitations, the fact remains that hundreds — thousands — have benefited from his foresight and public spirit. No one can argue with the writer who, shortly after Ferens' death, summed up his achievement. Ferens, he said, had lived 'a splendid, well-filled life of more than the allotted span, true to his ideals to the last'.

(William) Alfred Gelder
(1855-1941)
Architect and Civic Leader

Alfred Gelder is another of those great public figures who flourished in Victorian and Edwardian times. His story is a remarkable one of progress through ability, not privilege, and like so many of his contemporaries he showed intense commitment to the place where he lived and worked.

Alfred Gelder Street leaves no one in any doubt about the name of the man it honours. Having one's name attached to a street is as lasting a memorial as most people can hope to achieve. In this case it is particularly appropriate as Alfred Gelder was an architect and civic leader who played a major part in giving Hull some of its most important central streets.

Although Hull was the focus of his life, William Alfred Gelder (to give him his full name) was not a native of Hull. The Gelders were a North Cave family. His father, William, was a joiner and carpenter and the family home, where Alfred was born in 1855, was the attractive Georgian house at 30 Church Street.

In his professional role as an architect Alfred Gelder was responsible, either solely or with his partner Llewellyn Kitchen, for 'many of the City's largest emporiums, flour, and oil mills and Methodist churches'. War and demolition have inevitably had their impact: the old Market Hall he designed is one that has gone, but Paragon Arcade, which he planned and which opened in 1892, survives to celebrate its centenary.

But it is not so much in individual buildings as in the overall character and appearance of Hull that his influence is still felt. In the late 19th century Hull had an obvious need to create new thoroughfares and clear away decayed property, slums and narrow streets congesting its centre — at a time when the growth of both population and commercial activity was making the problem increasingly urgent. Alfred Gelder was well placed to play a leading role in the project. As well as being an architect he was also prominent on the Council, an alderman for many years, and mayor for a record five years in succession, 1898-1903. He was a tall, spare figure, and a characteristic pose was standing with his gold-rimmed spectacles in his hand as he addressed the Council.

Alfred Gelder Street, King Edward Street and Jameson Street were

Sir (William) Alfred Gelder and Lady Gelder.

(Humberside Leisure Services)

opened out to transform the appearance of the centre: the idea of broad avenues was extremely popular. Gelder himself favoured promenades and it is interesting to note that Alfred Gelder *Avenue* was the original suggestion for what was eventually designated as a mere street. 'Only those who remember old Hull can fully appreciate the broad streets with elegant buildings of imposing architectural design that have sprung up in the last quarter of a century,' wrote the local press in appreciation of Alfred Gelder's achievements. In his final year as mayor he was host to the Prince and Princess of Wales (the future George V and Queen Mary) when they made an official visit to Hull in 1903, and the knighthood he received shortly afterwards was attributed partly to this occasion, but also to his own contribution to the enhanced status of Hull as one of the great English cities.

By the 1930s Queen's Dock, a magnificent 18th-century project, had become unsuited to the needs of modern shipping, Monument Bridge was a frustrating time-waster to the much increased road transport, and Alfred Gelder was again involved in a radical scheme to infill the dock. As a result a valuable asset, a park in the centre of the City, was created, and Queen's Gardens was recognised as a lasting memorial to his vision and foresight. He was also an enthusiastic supporter of the idea of building a Humber bridge and worked tirelessly to make the dream a reality, but this was one plan he was never to see fulfilled.

Paragon Arcade.

Like Ferens, Gelder was a Wesleyan and consequently an important member of a group which exerted great influence in Hull. His professional and public duties were not, however, confined to the City, and in a crowded life he even found time to sit as Liberal M.P. for Brigg from 1910 to 1918, when, again like Ferens, he was defeated in the patriotic fervour of the 'Coupon Election' that followed the Armistice.

It can, of course, be difficult to discover the human being beneath the mass of titles and official positions which camouflage a public man. At the turn of the century phrenology was popular, and it is interesting that an Edwardian glossy, *The Hull Lady,* included a series of character studies of 'Hull's Public Men' by Professor Hatfield, a Bridlington phrenologist. Alfred Gelder, he deduced from a photograph, 'had dignity, firmness, perseverance, a great power of concentration', and, among an impressive list of other attributes, a keen sense of humour. His appearance indicated a man of action who worked 'with a view to improve men and things'. He had an analytical mind and approached problems logically: 'An untidy desk would not be in his line.'

Gelder lived for a long period at West Parade House, a very good address, and at least one person remembers the billiards room with its raised section for viewing the gentlemen at play.

He died in 1941 and the *Hull Daily Mail* summarised his achievements with admirable conciseness: He had, said an obituary notice, 'left Hull in a far better state than he found it.' Apart from the central layout of the City, and a street bearing his name, Hull possesses other interesting reminders of his life and work. There are portraits of himself and his wife in the Guildhall, a stained glass window in the Banqueting Chamber includes a tribute to him, and Holy Trinity Church has its fine Gelder Window (erected by his bequest in memory of his wife), a visual aid to the early history of Hull, depicting such men as Edward I and William de la Pole.

The simpler things, though, are often more evocative. Gelder and Kitchen continues as a leading firm of architects and their premises, appropriately one of Hull's historic buildings, Maister House, 160 High Street, still has Alfred Gelder's roll-top desk — a perfect memorial to a busy man who always kept his papers in order.

Charles Greenwood
(c.1757-1841)
Landlord of the Tiger Inn, Beverley

Another mystery man, known only through official records and indirect references. The human being, like most people, has evaded history, and, again like most, he was probably neither so good or so bad that he left an indelible impression on others. But one lives in hope: maybe some intriguing information still lurks in some unsuspected place.

Charles Greenwood is not a famous name in the history of Beverley. No picture of him appears to have survived, and it is most unlikely that his portrait was ever painted. He remains a faceless man. Yet in the period of around 35 years he lived in Beverley he must have been one of the town's best-known characters.

He was born c.1757, outside Yorkshire and quite possibly in Lincolnshire, but by 1798 at the latest he was landlord of the Beverley Arms, a coaching inn whose status was rivalled only by the nearby Tiger. It was a smart establishment and this was an auspicious time to take over. Previously the Blue Bell, it had been rebuilt in 1794 by William Middleton and renamed with the clear intention of staking its claim to be Beverley's leading inn. Ideally situated to attract passing trade, with plenty of space at the rear for stabling, it was the regular stop for coaches travelling between Hull and York, and, during 'the season', between Hull and Scarborough.

Whatever Greenwood's financial prospects, these early years at the Beverley Arms were devastated by personal disasters. His son, Thomas, born in January, 1798, died in November the same year. Three daughters then followed, Mary Ann in 1799, Sarah in 1800, and Charlotte in 1801. Mary Ann died in 1802 aged three, and Greenwood's 43-year-old wife, Mary, died the following year. It was a sad story, but infant mortality and the early death of mothers were common experiences in that period.

Greenwood was landlord of the Beverley Arms for something like ten years before he moved to the Fleece Inn, Louth, but he was back again in Beverley in February, 1815, when, perhaps surprisingly, he took over the Tiger, only a few yards north of his old establishment. Innkeepers, then as now, tried to pursue a course of upward mobility

(Tony Wharton)

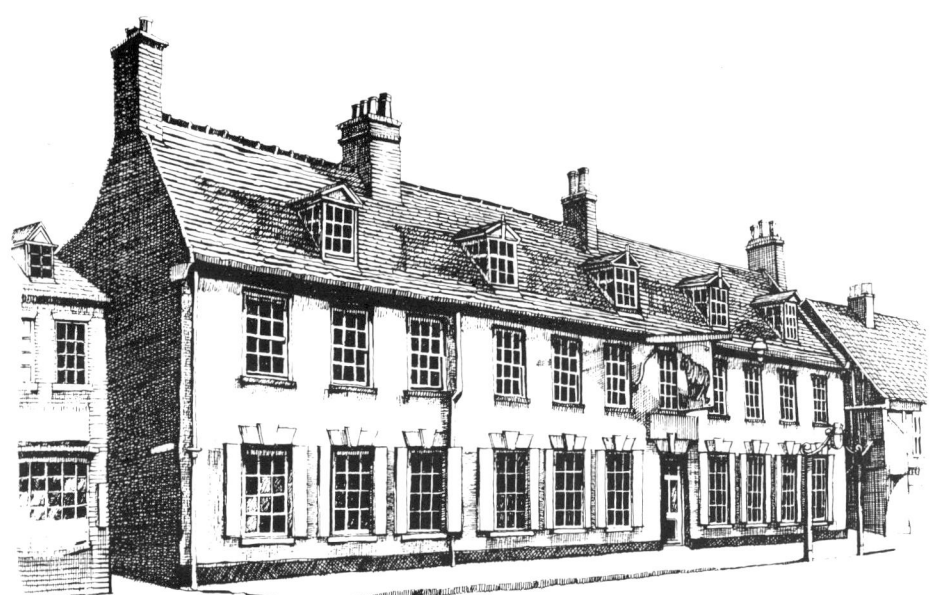

The Tiger, North Bar Within: its original appearance. Artist — Gary Sargeant.

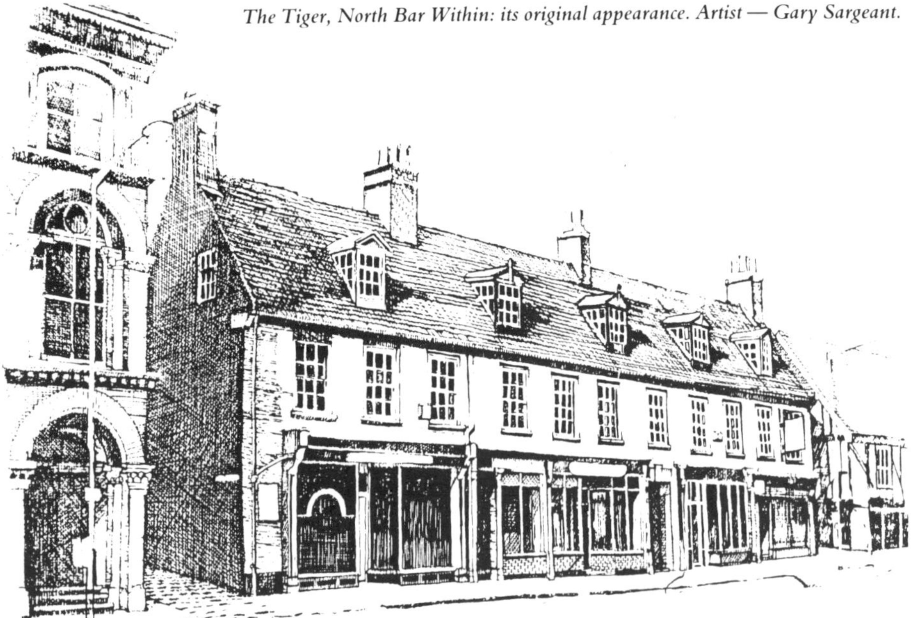

(Tony Wharton)

The Tiger after modern conversions. Artist — Gary Sargeant.

and the Tiger by this time may well have had the edge on the rival Beverley Arms as a well-appointed inn catering for an upper-class clientèle.

In a sonorously worded advertisement in two successive editions of the *Hull Advertiser* Charles Greenwood informed 'the nobility, gentry, commercial travellers and public in general' that he was to take over the Tiger on 20 February, 1815, 'and humbly solicits their patronage and support, assuring them no exertion shall be wanting to merit the same, by an unremitting attention to every department connected with their comfort and accommodation'.

There was certainly nothing inferior about the Tiger's facilities. As well as a spacious kitchen and extensive cellars it had six sitting or dining rooms (where well-to-do travellers ate in privacy), 16 bedrooms, a dormer storey of eight attics, and a fine first-floor room for the grandest functions. At the rear there was stabling for 40 horses and a complex of outbuildings: a brewhouse, wash house, laundry, ostlery and dairy. It was no mean inn of which to be landlord, and Charles Greenwood was to remain there for over 26 years.

During this period the Tiger was the venue of some memorable banquets. Culinary standards were high and Greenwood was prepared to pay high wages to secure the best staff. In 1828, when he advertised for an experienced cook, he stated that 'one completely mistress of her profession will be treated liberally'. One of the most splendid occasions must have been the dinner held to mark the coronation of Queen Victoria on 14 June, 1838, when the organising committee resolved: 'That the members of the Council and such gentlemen as chuse [sic] to join them on that day do dine at the Tiger Inn where tickets may be had price 4s. each. Dinner on table at 4 o'clock.'

One of the few certain facts known about Greenwood is that he was a horsey man. As well as being landlord of a major coaching house, he was also Clerk of the Course of the Holderness Hunt races, and the Tiger became the popular haunt of hunting and racing men. 'A number of highly respectable gentlemen' met at the inn in 1828 to form a hunting club for the East Riding and, business completed, 'A dinner was afterwards served in Mr. Greenwood's best style.' Facilities were also provided for gentlemen to have their horses seen by a veterinary surgeon who could be consulted at the inn every Wednesday and Saturday.

More information about Charles Greenwood could well be lurking in odd places awaiting discovery: to date only sparse personal details have come to light. He appeared in the census taken on 7 June, 1841, the first to record names as well as population figures. By then he was 84 but he had the support of his son, also Charles, in his mid-thirties, who lived with him.

Greenwood was lucky to be at the Tiger in its heyday during the golden age of coaching inns. Through his long years as landlord it was customary for Conservative candidates in Beverley's parliamentary elections to 'put up' at the Tiger, and noisy crowds would gather in North Bar Within to hear the speeches of the well-heeled politicians addressing them from the lofty eminence of the Tiger's first-floor windows.

Greenwood also provided accommodation for the meetings of local bodies ranging from the Constitutional Lodge of Freemasons to turnpike trustees and the clergy of the East Riding Archdeaconry. Auctioneers, too, used the Tiger for sales of property, and a celebrated visitor was Daniel O'Connell, the Irish 'Liberator', who addressed an audience of 100 in 1836.

Charles Greenwood died in October, 1841, and was spared the bitter experience of living through the Tiger's last days. In 1846 the railway came to Beverley and the coaching trade was fatally damaged. By 1847 Charles junior was facing serious financial problems — such a rapid decline that there must surely have been other factors at work. Had the running of the inn become slipshod in his father's declining years? Did Charles senior (maybe a gambling man) leave his son an inheritance of debt?

Whatever the reason, an auction was announced in July, 1847, of 'the whole of the household effects of Mr. Charles Greenwood, consisting of chairs, tables, featherbeds, sideboards, looking glasses, oil paintings, prints, window curtains, plates, *etc*', though in the event a general election was called and the inn was again used as headquarters by two candidates; contrary to custom, both were Liberal.

It was only a temporary postponement of the evil day, and in September, 1847, Greenwood junior's creditors forced a 'peremptory sale' of all his effects — sufficient, in fact, for a grand three-day auction, with a separate sale of his horses and carriages.

The Greenwood family thereafter disappear into oblivion, a poignant reminder of the speed with which the great characters of one generation become the forgotten people of the next.

Joseph Hind
(1816-1889)
Radical Councillor and Controversialist

Joseph Hind must have been an irritating man to know, with a persistent bee buzzing non-stop in his brain, and a disastrous lack of judgement which condemned him to pluck defeat from success and to make a perfect muddle of his private life. To contemporaries he may have been a pain, but today his faults can be forgiven.

When Joseph Hind died in 1889 the Liberal *Beverley Recorder,* to which he had been a major contributor, paid a glowing tribute to his virtues: 'For 40 years he had displayed incessant and unflagging energy in the cause of the people.'

In the interests of truth, no responsible editor could leave it at that: this was a case where it was impossible to speak only good of the dead. The writer of the obituary chose his words carefully but the meaning was unmistakable: 'There were many points in his character which must be described as unfortunate.' Joseph Hind was a brilliant man with a fatal flaw, a genius for making enemies as well as friends.

He was born on 3 September, 1816, in Butcher Row, Beverley, the son of John Hind, who supported a large family by working jointly as a shoemaker and cowkeeper. It was a modest background but it was claimed that the Hinds — originally Hynde and from Lincolnshire — had links with important people. A cousin, it was said, was High Sheriff of Lincolnshire and another kinsman was Bishop Green of Lincoln. Quite possibly belief in a more distinguished ancestry influenced Joseph, a comparatively poor man, to pursue the political path he chose to follow in Radical politics, attacking what he could not join.

About 1822 he became a pupil at the Anglican National School and by the age of 12 he was chief monitor — a kind of in-service training. There were times when the master was too drunk to teach and he was left in sole charge of the school of 250 children, an early experience of responsibility which no doubt provided a valuable, if awesome, exercise in acquiring self-confidence and showing initiative.

Joseph Hind loved the law — too much, in fact — but family circumstances never allowed him to qualify as a solicitor. As a second best, he became a clerk in the office of the Registrar of Deeds, was later promoted to the rank of chief clerk and in 1845 was appointed Deputy Registrar, being allowed to live rent-free in the Registrar's official residence (now part of the County Hall complex). When the Registrar died in 1882, the vacancy was filled, according to practice then current, by election. Joseph supported the successful candidate, George A. Thompson, who promptly broke his promise and dismissed him, a bitter experience which must have convinced him even more of the hostility of the world against which he was destined to battle.

Much of his most ferocious fighting took place in the Council Chamber. Hind, as a Radical councillor, was well to the left of the Liberal Party, totally fearless, a powerful orator and debater with a vigorous command of invective, and prepared to challenge all opposition in the pursuit of his convictions — whether he was right or wrong. He was a charismatic figure of extraordinary influence in Beverley with undeniable 'capacity for the management of public affairs', an outstandingly able chairman of the Finance Committee, and 'during two periods of its history he virtually ruled the town'.

The most controversial issue in late Victorian Beverley was the debate over the proposed supply of piped water, a reform which one might assume would have been welcomed by any progressive politician. But Hind, who believed in keeping the rates low and had a genuine concern for the poor who could not afford the cost of any new scheme, organised a ratepayers' association and campaigned successfully under the slogan, 'No waterworks, no half-crown rate',

Joseph Hind.

with the result that Beverley was slow to implement much-needed improvements in water supply and also in drainage.

Like so many public figures of his time, Joseph Hind, inspired by a real sense of moral responsibility, undertook an amazing burden of voluntary work. He ignored self-interest to the point of recklessness and devoted much of his time to improving the conditions and prospects of others, not least in education. He was closely involved in the Mechanics Institute, the organisation which provided education for working men in their limited free time, and he was a Guardian of the Poor; pursuing two objectives which do not always coincide, he 'rendered yeoman service to the needy and the ratepayers alike'. Another achievement was helping to establish the Foundation School in Albert Terrace (now the Health Centre) and he was a strong supporter of the Independent Chapel in Lairgate.

But it was his enthusiasm for attack, his keenness to begin an argument, which made him one of the town's characters. The late Philip Brown, the Beverley librarian who researched Hind's life and career, felt that the death of Hind's favourite son in 1864 may have been the turning point in his life, the traumatic experience which caused him such intense pain that he was impelled to vent his deep hurt on others.

His obsessional eagerness to go to law involved him in expenditure he could not afford and his financial position worsened. In his writing and speaking he was merciless towards his opponents, with 'a grievous fatality of putting himself in antagonism against those who were capable of rendering him service'. The local press provided a great outlet for his combative opinions and, in addition to his writing for the *Beverley Recorder,* he published for a time his own Radical paper, *The Beverley Freeman.* Philip Brown also speculated that Hind may have been the Beverley correspondent of the *Hull Advertiser.*

All these activities cost him time and, more seriously, most cost him money. He was not unique in being a man who was brilliant in managing public affairs but hopeless in personal matters. He earned a small income as sub-distributor of legal stamps, he became a school attendance officer, and he went in for speculative building in a small way in Westwood Road and Keldgate. His insatiable appetite for litigation, nevertheless, drove him towards inevitable bankruptcy and 'his later years were darkened by sorrow and privation'. He left his old stamping ground and went to live with his daughter in Plymouth, where he died in 1889.

Joseph Hind is certainly one of those characters in history who are pleasanter to read about than they were to live with. The eulogistic epitaphs on church memorials never quite ring true. It is much easier to have fellow-feeling for somebody who, like the rest of us, was far from perfect.

James Weir Hogg
(1790-1876)
Free-spending M.P. for Beverley

James Weir Hogg does not cut a very admirable figure in his appearances as a parliamentary candidate in Beverley but his entry in the Dictionary of National Biography *shows that he was a man of some ability who occupied and was offered a number of important posts. But what is really interesting is the glimpse he gives of the early stages in the history of a great political family.*

Beverley people loved elections. Not that they were particularly interested in politics, but an election meant an orgy of bribery and corruption, unlimited free drinking, free entertainment in the streets and plenty of opportunities and excuses for letting off steam in the carnival atmosphere that engulfed the town.

Hogg is a famous name in law and politics and James Weir Hogg, the great-grandfather of Quintin, Lord Hailsham, was an ideal candidate for Beverley when he stood as a Tory in 1835: ideal because he was a wealthy man and had no qualms about using his money to buy a seat at Westminster. He had made his fortune in India, and, when he returned home, he looked around for a likely constituency. Beverley, it seemed, was one where he was almost certain of success and on Christmas Eve, 1834, he introduced himself in a letter from his London house, 24 Bruton Street (not far from No. 17 where the Queen was born in 1926). In January, 1835, he arrived at the Tiger, North Bar Within, the fine coaching inn which served as headquarters for Tory candidates, with their Liberal opponents just down the road at the Beverley Arms.

A former M.P. had already told him 'that sometimes in very hot weather, perhaps in the dog days, the lads of Beverley were a little thirsty' and Hogg made a pledge: 'If the Beverlonians stick by me I will stick by them.' He was true to his word. Beverley had a bad reputation for electoral shenanigans but now it sank to new depths, and a critical newspaper complained that 'a more gross, or even ostentatious, display of corruption' had never been seen.

Predictably, Hogg topped the poll and had to suffer the doubtful honour of being 'chaired': carried in a ceremonial chair decorated with crimson ribbons (his party colours) and deposited back at the Tiger where he addressed the mob from an upstairs window. His supporters

Sir James Weir Hogg.

had nothing more to do but enjoy the 'flare-up' of their lives he had promised them.

A victorious candidate should keep in mind the next election. Hogg earned praise for his work at Westminster on behalf of the freemen whose 'just and undoubted rights' were secured by the Beverley Pastures Act and, more directly, he paid for a supply of coal and flour to be distributed to his 'friends' at the Dog and Duck as a Christmas gift in 1836. It proved a wise investment for the following year William IV died and, in accordance with custom at that period, Parliament was dissolved and a new one summoned by the new Queen, Victoria.

The electors of Beverley eagerly anticipated a fun-packed fortnight. Hogg and his Tory colleague, George Lane Fox (Beverley had two M.P.s), took up residence at the Tiger; the Tory inns, the Cross Keys, Green Dragon and White Horse, were full of happy drinkers, and bands paraded the streets from morning till ten at night sporting crimson colours.

Then the blow fell. The Liberal candidates, James Clay and George Rennie, announced their determination not to bribe but to take legal action against anyone who did.

Such shocking news 'fell upon the town like a great calamity' and the Tories tried to keep up their spirits by parading the streets, unaccompanied by musicians, as none could be hired, singing:

'Hogg, Hogg, fal de lal lay,
Hogg and Fox will win the day.'

Though his hands were banned from his pockets on this occasion, there was also a timely reminder of his habitual generosity:

'If you wish for flour and coal,
Vote for Crimson when you poll.'

Sufficient voters took the hint and, once again, Hogg ended in first place, with Fox not far behind.

The money he saved in 1837 came in useful at the next election four years later when a wealthy young Lancastrian, Charles Towneley, topped the poll by spending the massive sum of £8,000, while Hogg spent £6,000 to win the second seat. Years later Beverley voters recalled this halcyon time: 'There was money flying about the town, all through the town.'

It was Hogg's swansong in Beverley. He was created a baronet and at the next election stood successfully in Honiton. He had a large family, seven sons and seven daughters and, although the eldest son inherited the title and was promoted to the peerage, it was from his seventh son that his most famous descendants, Lord Hailsham and his father, both Lord Chancellors in their day, were descended.

Beverley certainly played a crucial part in the early stages of the family's remarkable ascent of the greasy pole of politics.

Joseph Malet Lambert
(1853-1931)

Clergyman, Social Reformer and Pioneer of Education

Heavily bearded Victorian clergymen look formidable figures, and their rigid views on religion and their unsmiling approach to life distance them from our own experiences. Joseph Malet Lambert was in many ways typical of these high-minded clerics, but he may have had hidden depths, now past recall.

Malet Lambert is a name immediately linked with a school — appropriately, too, because the man it honours was an influential figure in the history of education in Hull. Like the other men featured in this book, however, his public life had many facets, all of which deserve to be remembered.

One of the many valuable services performed by that excellent local historian, the late John M. Meadley, was rescuing from obscurity a number of distinguished 19th-century Hull clergy, and this account relies heavily on the result of his researches which appeared as a chapter in his work, *The Anglican Social Reformers Part III,* (again very fittingly) published as Number 3 in the Malet Lambert Local History Original series.

Joseph Malet Lambert, born in 1853, was the son of a Hull shipbroker, also Joseph, and his second wife, formerly Miss Jane Malet. His mother died when he was only a small child but, when he was 11, his father married again. Joseph junior's stepmother was Rachel née Wilson (sister of Arthur and Charles of the famous shipping firm) and by all accounts she was totally unlike her wicked fictional counterparts. According to oral evidence, Mrs. Lambert used to refer grandly to 'my husband, Malet', stressing the first syllable and giving the French pronunciation to the latter.

Although Joseph entered his father's business he had the urge to be ordained and took a degree at Trinity College, Dublin, before becoming curate at Tadcaster in 1879. When he was still only 28 he returned to Hull as vicar of St. John's, Newland, an appointment he held for over 30 years.

Malet Lambert was one of those remarkable Victorians who seem to have possessed inexhaustible stamina and a profound sense of duty to the community which made it impossible for them to restrict their

Canon Joseph Malet Lambert.

interests to one area of activity. Two of Malet Lambert's particular concerns were housing and sanitation, and his crusade to improve the living conditions of the ordinary people of Hull makes him a candidate eminently qualified to be enrolled among John Meadley's *Anglican Social Reformers.*

Nineteenth-century Hull experienced a dramatic rise in population along with increased industrialisation and trade, and far too many of its inhabitants were herded together in nauseous slums. Hull had a long history of failure to provide adequate supplies of pure water for its population, and remedying this unhealthy — and dangerous — state of affairs became one of Malet Lambert's principal campaigns.

For many years he was an influential member of the Hull Sanitary Association, and at the Hull Sanitary Congress held at the Town Hall in 1884 he made a speech which, even in printed form and after more than a century, rings with the passionate conviction of the speaker. Hull had its fine central streets, but behind them, hidden from public view and unknown to many, was a sub-world of depravity and despair which Malet Lambert brought before his audience in all its unlovely detail:

> 'There are about ten houses in each block built back to back, without drainage of any kind, rotten, filthy, the woodwork decayed, the windows often partly gone and replaced with old mats and hay. No wonder will be felt when I add that there are to be found there people, some of whom are as sad a disgrace to humanity as their dwellings are to the town in the centre of which they stand.'

But it was on education that he left his greatest mark. As chairman of Hull School Board he coped with a parsimonious committee and succeeded in bending the rules so that Hull obtained three excellent higher-grade schools, Brunswick Avenue, Craven Street, and the Boulevard, which, in effect, provided secondary education, although the existing constitution did not allow expenditure for such a purpose. The reputation of these schools was so great that old pupils still mention them with pride.

When school boards were abolished and their functions taken over by local authorities, Malet Lambert became chairman of Hull Corporation's Higher Education Sub-Committee. In addition, he played a major role in the foundation of Hull University and was the first chairman of the University College's Council. Some of Malet Lambert's most important educational work, for which people today have reason to be grateful, was his campaign for a public library service. Although councils were empowered to levy a rate to provide library facilities, Hull was reluctant to take the necessary step. Eventually, convinced by James Reckitt's initiative in East Hull, it did so, and Malet Lambert became deputy chairman and, later, chairman of the Library Committee.

All these voluntary extra-mural activities were, of course, subsidiary to the parish work which was his first priority. He was responsible for important alterations at St. John's, which included a new chancel, extending the west end, and adding a north aisle. The population of Newland was increasing and it was rapidly losing its original rural character, so much so that Malet Lambert was convinced of the need to subdivide the large parish; ultimately he succeeded and St. Augustine's in Queens Road was consecrated in 1896. His status as a leading figure in the Anglican Church was officially recognised by his successive appointments as Rural Dean of Hull, Canon of York Minster, and Archdeacon of the East Riding.

Those who complain about their stressful lifestyle in the 1990s can only wonder at the amount of work and responsibility such men as Malet Lambert managed to undertake. After his appointment to St. John's he took further degrees, becoming a Doctor of Laws in 1885, he contributed articles to the local press, was a supporter of the early trade unions and, as an academic, wrote *Two Thousand Years of Gild Life*, published in 1891. Eventually he became an alderman on the East Riding County Council.

One sad, uncharacteristic, episode in an otherwise distinguished public career was a charge brought against him and his wife, accused in 1909 of ill-treating a child in their custody. There was great popular relief and rejoicing when they were found not guilty.

In 1912 he left Hull for Bridlington but the move made little difference to his close involvement in the affairs of the City. Active to the end, he died in 1931, and, as a perfect postscript to his long life of public service, it was decided that when Craven Street School, which he had been instrumental in creating, moved to new premises in 1932, it should take the name of Malet Lambert.

William Middleton
(1730-1815)
Builder of Georgian Beverley

The late K. A. MacMahon had a high regard for Middleton and it was his lectures which first interested me, and I suspect many others, in this important Georgian builder. It is difficult to get at any significant details about Middleton the man but he has left a lasting impact on the appearance of Beverley.

Above the fireplace in the Magistrates' Room in Beverley Guildhall hangs a not particularly distinguished portrait of an amiable-looking man. It is, however, right that it should have a place of honour in the town's civic centre because the man it depicts, William Middleton, not only built the Guildhall but also had a lasting impact on the appearance and character of Beverley.

Middleton, born in 1730, was apprenticed to a joiner, Samuel Smith, a wise career move at just the right time. Beverley was then enjoying a renaissance after the ravages of the Civil War and a long period of economic decline by being transformed into an elegant town where people of adequate means could live in attractive houses and indulge in a variety of civilised pleasures. There was plenty of work and opportunities for builders, and a Georgian joiner could do far more than his modest description suggested: men like Middleton could build to their own designs.

A town with aspirations of grandeur required an appropriately fine building where public affairs could be discussed. The Tudor Guildhall was in poor condition, in 1762 the Corporation decided to re-build on the same site, and William Middleton's plans and estimates were duly accepted. The building he produced was as grand as any Beverley alderman could ever have envisaged and it was given the crowning touch by the Italian stuccoist, Guiseppe Cortese, who created the magnificent ceiling with its figure of Justice unblindfolded, and the royal coat of arms behind the mayoral dais.

At the same time Middleton was involved in another major building scheme. Georgian ladies and gentlemen took great delight in displaying themselves prominently at smart social functions — readers of Jane Austen will recall the pleasure some of her characters took in 'quizzing' [commenting critically on] others who had put themselves

William Middleton.

Beverley Arms, formerly the Blue Bell, rebuilt by Middleton 1794.

Nos. 55-65 North Bar Within, Beverley, probably built by Middleton.
40 North Bar Within, Beverley, another of Middleton's buildings.

on public display. In 1761 Middleton started building Assembly Rooms where the *glitterati* of Beverley could participate in such communal pleasures. On this occasion he worked to the designs of the great John Carr of York on the site now occupied by the Regal. Middleton was a prominent man in Beverley, four times elected mayor, and often worked for the Corporation. Two of his public buildings were the Fish Shambles of 1777 behind his former master, Samuel Smith's, earlier Butchers' Shambles, and he also Georgianised the Blue Bell and turned it into the more dignified Beverley Arms Hotel.

Much of his work, however, was on a smaller scale, building reasonably-sized attractive houses for reasonably well-off residents. Beverley's eminent historian, the late K. A. MacMahon, made an important point when he explained the limitations within which Middleton had to operate. 'He found no noble patron to make easier for him the possibility of experiment,' he wrote. 'His customers for the most part were hard-headed senators and middle-class townsmen' who disapproved of ostentation and over-spending.

A fine pair of Middleton houses, now used as offices, are Nos. 72-4 Lairgate, and other surviving examples of his work include No. 39 North Bar Without, No. 40 North Bar Within, No. 1 Saturday Market, No. 2 Highgate, and Nos. 6-8 Butcher Row. Stylistic similarities, however, show his hand in far more than these. Local pride should not mislead us into crediting him with architectural genius. Like other builders of his time he used pattern books and there was nothing particularly original in his designs. But his buildings were pleasant, civilised and well-proportioned, often with impressive entrances.

Middleton has links with a well-known East Riding family. In 1795 his daughter, Margaret, married John Hall, and their son, James Middleton Hall, the squire of Scorborough, financed the building of Scorborough Church and was Master of the Holderness Foxhounds for 30 years. James' wife was Sarah, daughter of Richard Watt of Bishop Burton, and their grandson, who changed his name to Hall-Watt, eventually united the two estates.

William Middleton, as Ken MacMahon commented, was a man who built 'stolidly utilitarian' buildings but he was a designer of whom Prince Charles would approve. His buildings were ideal for the people who were to occupy them and they were ideal for their environment. Who could ask for more?

James Craig Niven
(1828-1881)
Botanist and Garden Designer

In the years I spent at Hymers I never once heard a mention of James Niven but my interest in him, which began with a realisation that he had been responsible for landscaping Pearson Park, has rapidly grown into hero worship and opened up a whole new area of history to me. I now know that he came from a line of distinguished gardeners and botanists and Hull was lucky to have the services of a man of such talent.

James Niven is not a name that means much to local people, yet he was a man of remarkable talent whose achievement is still visible in Hull. He was a Victorian landscape gardener and two examples of his work survive in the City: Pearson Park and (to some extent) in Hymers College grounds, formerly the Botanic Gardens.

James Craig Niven was the third generation of a family of eminent gardeners. His Scottish grandfather, also James (1774-1827), was in charge of the Royal Botanic Gardens, Edinburgh, and his father, Ninian (1799-1879), was Curator of the Botanic Gardens, Dublin. It was in Ireland that *his* son, Hull's James Niven, was born in 1828.

Only 25 when he arrived in Hull in January, 1853, he had already distinguished himself as a gardener and botanist. He had obviously inherited the Nivens' horticultural genes and, following two years training at the Royal Botanic Gardens, Belfast, he worked for the Duke of Buccleuch, and in 1847 moved to Kew. At the age of 19 he was promoted to a senior post and in 1852 made Assistant Curator.

A year later the Director of Kew was asked for help in finding a new Curator for Hull's troubled Botanic Gardens. There were 50 candidates, and Niven was selected.

Hull's gardens had been opened on Anlaby Road in 1812 as the exclusive preserve of upper-middle-class members with an interest in botany. So sacred were its precincts that members' children were forbidden entry when accompanied by mere servants. Unfortunately, such an élitist policy resulted in a lack of popular support and inadequate income, and Niven immediately made his influence felt by remodelling the grounds. After two or three years battling against 'a deep-rooted spirit of exclusiveness on the part of the Committee of

James Craig Niven.

Management' he had achieved such a thorough reorganisation that the membership had trebled, and the gardens' huge collection of plants gave them national status.

When Zachariah Charles Pearson decided to mark his mayoralty by donating an entry-free park, the project offered Niven superb scope for letting his imagination soar and create a garden which fulfilled his artistic aspirations. Pearson Park may have risen on the shaky foundation of Pearson's generosity but from the débacle of his later bankruptcy Hull acquired a garden which reflected Niven's romantic vision: a landscape more picturesque than Nature could manage, with a lake fringed with trees drooping their boughs in the water, curving gently, dreamily into the distance.

Niven seems to have had an urge to fill every minute with activity. He delivered three lectures each week to students of the School of Medicine and during his years in Hull he delivered a staggering total of 38 courses of lectures to learned bodies. He also contributed articles to journals and edited a six-volume work on botanic gardens. He was keen to encourage poor people to enjoy gardening, even if they had only a window box, and his ideas aroused such interest that he prepared a pamphlet of instructions.

Hull's first Botanic Gardens, Anlaby Road, 1812-77.

Hull's second Botanic Gardens, Spring Bank West, 1880-1890; the grounds of Hymers College from 1893.

(Hymers College)

The family home can hardly have been a quiet retreat. The 1871 Census shows Niven, then 42, living there with his wife Elizabeth (39), five sons and a daughter (from 16 to a few weeks). A servant, the foreman-gardener, and a 13-year-old apprentice gardener also lived in.

In spite of Niven's efforts, the Botanic Gardens were doomed to decline. Hull was expanding at a prodigious rate and the six-acre site, where select parties had once spent pleasant hours 'beneath the old oaks, listening to the warble of the birds and enjoying the cool shade', suffered under an increasingly powerful onslaught of noise and smoke from the streets developed on all sides.

The rural ambience was impossible to retain, Niven's evergreens suffered more each year, and the gardens closed in 1877. The entrance was in Linnaeus Street (commemorating the great botanist) and only the name carries a faint echo of past glories.

Niven, happily, had one more opportunity for displaying his talents in Hull. A much larger site, of over 50 acres, was acquired on Spring Bank West, and he was commissioned to design new Botanic Gardens on a far grander scale. This time a romantically curved lake had an inset island and banks surrounded by rhododendrons 'and other showy plants', and he devised a sophisticated layout of bushes and labyrinthine walks to avoid any suggestion of a dull geometrical pattern. As a gardener of vision he looked to the future and planted shrubs and saplings that would one day form a woodland setting.

For James Niven, however, there was to be little future. All this demanding work must have been a drain on his constitution and he was now paying the price. The gardens were opened on 19 July, 1880, and 53-year-old Niven died at the Curator's house on 16 October, 1881, after a long illness, but still 'in harness'.

Obituaries praised his kindness, his gift for friendship, his untiring energy, and the 'profit and the pleasure' he had given to many inhabitants of Hull. The new Botanic Gardens, it was believed, would 'remain a monument to his unceasing labours'.

In the following years more free parks opened — West Park in 1885 and East Park in 1887 — and the Botanic Gardens, which could never quite reconcile their dual aims of pleasure and scientific study, closed in 1890.

There is, fortunately, a sequel which ends the story on a happier note. Hull was about to acquire a new school, and the redundant gardens proved an ideal site for Hymers College, which opened in 1893.

Part of Niven's lake survives, many of his trees and shrubs still flourish, and in a dry summer the foundations of the bandstand can still be traced. Conversion into school grounds has preserved an important green oasis not too far from the city centre.

Niven has no statue, but none is needed. His gardens are the finest memorial he could have.

Zachariah Charles Pearson
(1821-91)
Shipowner and Public Benefactor

Larger-than-life figures are liable to have major defects as well as outstanding virtues. You have to take them as they are: the good and the bad cannot be separated. Pearson's financial ventures may have been shady and his display of public generosity not all it appeared, but out of it came something valuable.

Hull has often had a bad press. But even its critics have to admit that one feature distinguishes it from the stereotyped northern town: the attractive approach roads with neat grass verges and central areas planted with flowers and trees.

Hull's reputation for public gardens is nothing new, though the earliest ones were not open freely to all. Only subscribers were admitted to the Botanic Garden (opened 1812) and there was an admission charge to the Zoological Gardens (opened 1840).

Pearson Park, a picturesque corner of Victorian England, which remains — one hopes — forever in Hull, was the first to which everyone had free access. All the Hull parks are attractive and interesting, but Pearson Park has another claim to attention. Behind its idyllic scenery lies a story of high drama. Nineteenth-century Hull was rapidly expanding and had a growing need for a park where the working classes could relax from their labours. Zachariah Charles Pearson, Hull's 39-year-old mayor, was keen to mark his year of office, 1859-60, in a spectacular way and gave the land for the long-desired park.

He was a self-made man but far from typical. The traditional account of his early life reads like fiction. Born in 1821 and orphaned at four, he stowed away, so it is said, when he was 12 but was discovered and brought home. Still determined to go to sea, he approached a captain and asked, 'Please, sir, do you want a boy?' He was taken on as an apprentice and did so well that at 21 he was a captain. His career gathered momentum and he became a merchant and a shipowner with a splendid fleet of steamers. Such dazzling progress had rarely been equalled — anywhere — and he advanced just as rapidly in civic life, going swiftly through the ranks of councillor, alderman, sheriff (in 1858) and mayor for the first time in 1859. In spite of his thrusting career, he somehow acquired the suave manner of a man-about-town and showed 'no trace of the gruff, surly sea captain' which might have been expected.

Business success was not enough, and even his mayoralty had to be exceptional. Accordingly he purchased 37 acres of land for £7,400 and gave 27 of the acres for a park. The ten acres he retained for building houses were on the perimeter, and the Local Board of Health undertook to make a road round the park and provide lighting — which, Pearson later agreed, considerably increased its value. When

Zachariah Charles Pearson.

Statue of Prince Albert, 1868.

Statue of Queen Victoria, 1863.

Alderman W. H. Moss expressed the town's gratitude ('A nobler, more generous, more magnificent gift he could not imagine!') he was warmly cheered, even though some, jealous of Pearson's meteoric rise, muttered cynically about his motives.

On 27 August, 1860, Hull was in carnival mood for the opening of what was often called 'The People's Park'. Shops were closed, flags flew, 19 boats ferried 10,000 spectators into Hull and over 20,000 came by train to watch a procession which took 45 minutes to pass. At a grand ceremony in the new park Pearson signed the deed of conveyance and planted the first tree and, after a day of festivities, was host at a magnificent formal dinner at the Royal Station Hotel. He commissioned sculptor Thomas Earle to make a statue of Queen Victoria and he was acclaimed as 'the people's friend and the working man's benefactor'.

Half way through his second period as mayor, 1861-2, his world collapsed with stunning finality.

Pearson had been tempted to aim even higher and become the greatest shipowner in Hull. It was the time of the American Civil War. He bought, on credit, a large fleet of ships and attempted 'to run arms through the Federal blockade'. His gamble failed. On one terrible day in the summer of 1862 he read in *The Times* that a ship he had agreed to sell for £35,000 had been destroyed by fire. He arrived at his office and heard that two of his vessels had been captured. He returned home £85,000 poorer. Later came news that almost all his ships had been taken. It was a fall as terrible as that of the Mayor of Casterbridge. Pearson was bankrupt and resigned as mayor and alderman. He obtained employment as a ship's surveyor, and when he died in 1891 he had lived for 30 years in obscurity in a modest house in a corner of the park which bore his name.

In time most things can be forgiven. He left a wonderful legacy: a large, landscaped park surrounded by fine villas, with a graceful, quite rare, statue of Queen Victoria as a young woman, seated: Alderman Moss, who had so fulsomely praised Pearson, settled the bill, for Pearson had only paid Earle £100. A fine statue of Prince Albert, 'The Good', also by Earle, erected by the grateful people of Hull, and a charming water fountain, a splendid conservatory, and impressive gates were later added. A prehistoric ironstone pillar now bears a relief of Pearson's profile and, nearby, is the cupola of the now demolished Victorian Town Hall for which Pearson had been an enthusiastic campaigner — an ironic symbol!

On a sunny day, at any time of year, the park is an attractive oasis of which any city could be proud. When Pearson saw the trees maturing and his vision achieving reality, perhaps bitter memories were occasionally replaced by moments of consolation.

George Frederick Samuel Robinson, Earl de Grey and Ripon
(1827-1909)
Unseated M.P. and High Steward of Hull

Earl de Grey I find a particularly fascinating character because of the way his life evolved. He remained true to his political views but it is difficult to see the respected statesman in the young man who stood as a candidate in the Hull election of 1852, and in religion he moved away from his early beliefs.

Earl de Grey and Ripon means different things to different people in Hull.

A pub and a street are named after the first part of his title. There is also a Ripon Way, and in the past there was Ripon Street, Ripon Terrace and Ripon Grove as well as Ripon Villas, the Ripon Arms and the Ripon Hall. Obviously a man who has left his mark on the city! Yet the honour in which he was eventually held is rather ironical, for his first official encounter with Hull was nothing to boast about.

To be an earl is to belong to a select group, but two earldoms put you in a distinctly small minority. He began with the straightforward name of George Frederick Samuel Robinson, but from the first he was exceptional. At the time of his birth in 1827 his father, Viscount Goderich, was Prime Minister and so he was one of that exclusive group born at 10 Downing Street. When Goderich became Earl of Ripon in 1833, his son automatically took over the courtesy title of viscount.

He was, therefore, Lord Goderich when he appeared in Hull in 1852 to stand as Liberal Candidate in a general election. He was only 24 and obviously, if elected, would one day have to transfer from the Commons to the Lords, but this could be a canny move on the part of Hull. The Upper House had far more power than it does today and, as a local newspaper pointed out, an ex-Hull M.P. there would give the town 'real representation' in the Lords.

Hull at that time had two M.P.'s, who together represented the entire town, and the other Liberal candidate, James Clay, M.P. since 1847, was decidedly lukewarm about Goderich's standing. When they met in London it was made unmistakably clear that Goderich should bear the major part of the considerable expenses involved and, further, if the Liberals could return only one man, it was to be Clay.

Earl de Grey and Ripon, later Marquis of Ripon.

The unveiling of the statue of Edward I in the new Town Hall, 1866, by Earl de Grey, High Steward of Hull.

(Humberside Leisure Services)

Naturally Clay's main concern was keeping his seat, but another issue divided them. Goderich was far more Radical than Clay, and his Christian Socialist views had proved too extreme for other constituencies. 'I feel every day how widely I differ from all existing parliamentary parties,' he wrote to Thomas Hughes, author of *Tom Brown's Schooldays*. 'As to my prospects [in Hull], I am not the man to represent the middle classes, although in all commercial and financial questions I ought to please them.'

Nevertheless, he duly arrived in Hull, an unassuming academic figure thrust into a hectic campaign notorious for its bribery and corruption. His appearance, a journalist noted, 'was altogether indicative of a well-bred unaffected English nobleman.' His stature was small, his clothing simple, and, being short-sighted but not wearing spectacles, he 'laboured under some disadvantage'.

Any physical and most political defects could be offset in Hull by an adequate supply of money for bribery, though on occasions Goderich was said to be 'rendered a little uneasy by the mysterious methods of his agents', and 'extraordinary demands' made on his pocket. Lady Goderich came to help in his canvass and the couple stayed at W. T. Palmer's house in Albion Street. A Conservative elector claimed that a box of gold was delivered there from the railway station and, later, a mysterious stream of voters was observed going down the area steps and emerging through the front door in never-ending succession from 10 p.m. to 2 a.m. 'It is not very likely that they came out empty-handed,' he commented.

In spite of inexperience on a platform and a treble-voice, Goderich put his views forward courageously — if patronisingly by modern standards. 'I am not afraid, gentlemen, of my fellow countrymen,' he told them. 'I have no fear of those who dwell in what have been termed the lowest quarters, for I am proud to say that I number among my friends men of all classes and even inhabitants of those low and vulgar quarters.'

Both Clay and Goderich were elected by large majorities and 400 'gentlemen' attended a celebratory banquet at the Assembly Rooms. But their triumph was short-lived. The Tories petitioned against the result and on 7 March, 1853, judgment was given: bribery and treating by their agents had cost Clay and Goderich their seats. A Royal Commission of Inquiry then sat for 57 days, making a thorough investigation into Hull's elections and producing a massive condemnation of the way they were conducted.

Such an occurrence today would almost certainly end the political career of anyone involved, but the working men of Hull formed committees to organise 'testimonials of esteem' of the two unseated Members, and Goderich was given a richly-chased silver tankard in gratitude for his role as 'the firm advocate and faithful guardian of the political rights of the people'. In 1857 Clay was re-elected and served Hull, a popular hero, until his death, while Goderich went on to represent Huddersfield from 1853-7 and then the West Riding until 1859 when he succeeded his father as Earl Ripon and his uncle as Earl de Grey. In his first campaign Earl de Grey (as we shall now call him) had been a novice, but he quickly matured and gained a high reputation as a public speaker. In 1859 he joined the Cabinet as Under Secretary for War, still only in his early 30s.

The Marquis of Normanby, High Steward of Hull, died in 1863 and the Corporation clearly thought this a good time to renew old links with Earl de Grey. Accordingly he was offered, and accepted, the vacant honorary appointment.

The day on which he was installed as High Steward, 29 October, 1863, was one of those public festivities from which the Victorians derived every ounce of pleasure possible. Earl de Grey arrived by train the day before and drove to Brunswick House where he was to be the guest of Henry Blundell. The following morning, 'at early dawn', he was one of a dazzling band of local celebrities who congregated at Samuelson's shipyard ('Sammy's Point') for an exceptional event, the launch of four ships, one named 'Earl de Grey and Ripon' and another 'Countess of Ripon'. After a champagne breakfast, Earl de Grey, Deputy Grand Master of English Freemasons, was made an honorary

Earl de Grey, Castle Street, Hull.

member of the Humber Lodge, and then a procession of fellow masons accompanied him to Trinity House where he was made an honorary brother.

The climax was, of course, his installation as High Steward and the whole ceremony was an oratorical extravaganza, with sufficient flattering comments from everyone involved to dispel 'all unpleasant reminiscences in his lordship's mind of what took place a few years ago'. It ended with immense cheering, and Earl de Grey and other notables then entered their carriages and drove to Pearson Park by a deliberately circuitous route. The weather was unkind but the crowds undeterred. Most businesses had closed at 1 p.m. and thousands of spectators lined the flag-decorated streets to watch the procession pass by. Hearty cheers greeted the Earl but there can have been nothing more remarkable on view than an 'ornamental car' drawn by four grey horses, and on it 'a light and elegant temple', inside which were allegorical figures representing the four Continents, Peace and Plenty.

Earl de Grey's first public duty as High Steward was to unveil the statue of Queen Victoria in Pearson Park, originally commissioned by Zachariah Pearson himself and now, after an embarrassing hiatus caused by his bankruptcy, having the balance owing to the sculptor discreetly settled by the Mayor, W. H. Moss.

It had been intended to take full advantage of the new High Steward's presence by asking him to lay the foundation stone of South Bridge ('Ha'penny Bridge') but insufficient progress had been made and the great day ended with yet another banquet in the Assembly Rooms. There were still more honours in store for the Earl and he amassed a glittering list of appointments: Under Secretary to the India Board, Lord President of the Council, Governor General of India, First Lord of the Admiralty and Secretary for the Colonies. He was made a Knight of the Garter, awarded two honorary doctorates, and in 1871 raised to an even loftier rank as Marquis of Ripon.

A photograph taken in later life shows the face of a man of strong character, wise and kind — nothing like the lightweight candidate of 1852. His Radical views had become even firmer and he continued to campaign for the causes to which he was committed, particularly Home Rule for Ireland and educational opportunities for all. 'I started at a high level of Radicalism. I am a Radical still,' he said not long before his death in 1909.

One step he took had a major impact on his public life. From 1871 he was Grand Master of the Freemasons, but resigned in 1874 when he was received into the Catholic Church.

After a shaky start in 1852, he had made a quick recovery and enjoyed a long career of distinguished service. Perhaps Hull was right, after all, to hold him in such high esteem.

Dr. Thomas Sandwith
(1791-1867)
Doctor and Public Servant

Thomas Sandwith is difficult to fault. He was a distinguished public figure, and, when circumstances brought him into contact with a famous patient, the surviving evidence shows him as a humane and sympathetic doctor.

Dr. Thomas Sandwith's memorial in St. Mary's Church, Beverley, carries a glowing tribute to his character and his life's work. He died, so it claims, 'greatly honoured and sincerely regretted, after a long life spent in the service of others'.

It was no polite over-statement. Sandwith was one of those remarkable men who made a significant contribution to local life in the 19th century. Although he performed a busy round of professional duties, he also took on a formidable list of unpaid voluntary tasks.

He was born at Helmsley in 1791 into an eminent local family whose former residence, Bankings House, was incorporated into the Black Swan Hotel after the Second World War. The Sandwiths were upper-middle-class people, and male members of the family followed successful careers in law, medicine and the army. When Thomas was four his parents moved to a house in North Bar Within and, after attending Beverley Grammar School, he was sent to London for his medical training. The sudden death of his father abruptly ended his studies and he came home to Beverley. Doctors were less strictly controlled in the early 19th century than they are today and Sandwith apparently began practising when he was only 18. The 1841 census shows him living with his large family at Highgate House, Wednesday Market (now occupied by Lockings, Solicitors).

As well as being a hard-working doctor he entered enthusiastically into local politics, motivated by the determination to improve conditions for those less privileged than himself, and he was also active in bringing Liberal candidates forward in parliamentary elections. A member of Beverley Borough Council, he was three times mayor, in 1837, 1846 and 1852, and in his later years he was regarded as Beverley's grand old man of the Liberal Party.

Sandwith kept up a keen interest in science and other intellectual pursuits and supported 'every society tending to the elevation of the

Dr. Thomas Sandwith.

working classes and benefit of the town'. He was intimately involved in the Mechanics Institute, and he frequently lectured to its members. In addition, he was a J.P. and a Charitable Trustee — altogether a roll of honour of public service willingly undertaken. Today he would probably be dismissed as a 'do-gooder'.

For 54 years he was surgeon at the East Riding House of Correction and, although Robert Peddie, one of the inmates there in the early 1840s, must have tried the patience of a man who had more tolerance than most, Dr. Sandwith's neat, handwritten record of the treatment he administered (now in the Public Record Office, Kew) is unselfconscious but impressive evidence of his kindness and concern.

Peddie, a Scottish staymaker and a prominent Chartist — a supporter of the People's Charter which advocated such reforms as granting every man a vote, then considered revolutionary — had been sentenced to three years' hard labour for his part in a riot in Bradford, a charge he strenuously denied. He was sent to Beverley to serve his sentence and, as a man who claimed to be a political prisoner, not a criminal, he rebelled against the severity of the prison regime.

His most presistent grievance was the humilitation and physical suffering caused by the treadmill, used in Beverley to crush chalk into whiting. Male prisoners had to 'tread the mill' for periods of 20 minutes, the equivalent of climbing 1,100 steps on an endless staircase, before being allowed a ten-minute rest. This punishing routine was followed three times before breakfast, six times between breakfast and dinner, and nine times between dinner and supper. It was cruel labour and Peddie complained bitterly of 'the perspiration dropping from his forehead and body like heavy drops in a shower of rain' and the consequent giddiness, blurred vision and nausea.

Sandwith was a man of his time, conditioned by current attitudes, and, as a prison surgeon, he accepted the use of the treadmill. But within these limits he was remarkably understanding of Peddie's problems and did not regard them as the mere moans of a malcontent. On a number of occasions he allowed him extra food, tea and sugar, and, as he recorded: 'I was doubtful whether the prison diet was sufficient for a man of his size and habits of life.' Peddie was granted an additional half-pound of oatmeal and a quart of milk daily, and there was a whole catalogue of treatments dispensed for a variety of ills. Even Peddie, not the easiest of patients, acknowledged the way his suffering had been alleviated. The £60 p.a. pension which Sandwith was awarded after 54 years' devoted duty was surely deserved.

A life of service in so many spheres eventually affected his health and his heart showed signs of weakness. On 1 March, 1867, he was extremely ill and advised to rest, and a warning telegram sent to his brother, Dr. Humphry Sandwith, in Hull. He ignored the cautions and, with renewed vigour, continued to visit patients until a short time before his death on 3 March. He was 75.

Great praise was showered on a man who was 'a gentleman in the strictest sense of the word' and who had been 'a true and valued friend to the poor'. The simplest words, however, are often the most moving. Dr. Sandwith was, one newspaper reported, 'literally worn out'.

It was the perfect epitaph for a great public servant.

Daniel Sykes
(1776-1832)
The Reluctant M.P. for Hull and Beverley

Daniel Sykes is another of my heroes, a man of outstanding principle and integrity who longed for privacy but became an M.P. out of a sense of duty. He had no aspirations to be colourful in the literal sense of the word but his high standards are a shining light in a grey world of mediocrity and half-truths.

People who pass through the impressive foyer of Hull's City Hall may never even notice the statue of Daniel Sykes wearing a Roman-style toga. It stands in a corner, out of the limelight, a position he would have liked for, although he led a public life, he was a very private man. His fine residence at Raywell, a discreet distance from the road, is a house with the quiet dignity of the man himself.

Both house and its original owner deserve to be better known. The Sykes of Sledmere are famous, but the other branch of the family, the Sykes of Westella, also played an important part in local life. Both branches are descendants of Richard Sykes (1658-1728), a merchant in High Street, Hull, which he made the East Riding base of the family. The Sykes had been cloth merchants in Leeds and this was a well-chosen move at a time when Hull was poised for expansion. As Hull prospered, so did the Sykes.

Richard married twice. His first wife, Mary Kirby, produced an heir and brought Sledmere into the family, but his second wife, Martha Donkin, was the mother of Joseph (1723-1805), in turn the father of Daniel of Raywell.

Joseph was another prosperous High Street merchant. He was twice mayor of Hull and, once, its sheriff, but, following a well-trodden route, in 1756 he moved his home from the commercial source of his wealth to a country estate, Westella Hall.

Daniel (born 1776) was his fifth son. He went to Pocklington School where he formed a friendship with William Wilberforce which was to have lasting consequences. At Cambridge, rather uncharacteristically, he was drawn into a set of dissolute students but, much truer to form, quickly saw the light. He then studied for the bar and, although he suffered all his life from poor health, refused Joseph's financial inducements to give up law. Realising, however, that he could never

Daniel Sykes when young.

Statue of Daniel Sykes in the City Hall, formerly in the Mechanics Institute.

stand the strain of a London practice, he joined the provincial circuit and had chambers at 16 Bowlalley Lane, Hull. In 1821 he became Recorder of Hull.

Daniel's marriage to Isabella Wright of Stamford Bridge was a happy one, though childless. Joseph had bought a farmhouse called Raywell (sometimes Shardale) in 1803, and when he died two years later it passed to Daniel, who built the present house, designed by Marmaduke Pycock of Wakefield.

At Raywell House Daniel lived in the quietly civilised style which suited his gentle personality. The house was comfortable and well-ordered but in no way ostentatious. Daniel did not like idling away time at dinner parties in 'hollow conversation'. The fine food and wine he could well afford did not interest him and he even said that he would have preferred to be spared the trouble of eating and drinking. Part of the evening's entertainment at Raywell was reading poetry. Literature gave him great pleasure, and he was fluent in Italian and French.

Altogether Daniel may sound a cold fish. Yet George Pryme M.P., who knew him better than most, made a perceptive comment. 'Beneath a cold exterior,' he wrote, one would find 'the strong glow of feeling and a heart warm with affection.'

Even so, his introverted nature hardly made him an ideal parliamentary candidate in a period when elections were often drunken orgies, rife with corruption. Yet he served 11 years as a distinguished M.P.

His public life was strongly influenced by his upbringing. The Sykes of Westella were people with a deep social conscience, aware of their duty to use their privileged position to help others. Unlike their cousins at Sledmere, they were Whigs, committed to reform — and their wealth gave them the independence to promote their progressive ideas with no need to kow-tow to superiors. Joseph Sykes was the great-great-grandfather of E. M. Forster, author of *A Passage To India,* who inherited a small part of the fortune and a full measure of the liberal principles of his Hull ancestors.

The toga on Daniel's statue in Hull was appropriate for a man who loved the classics, but not for one who supported causes which were often in advance of public opinion. He believed that everyone was entitled to education and that more men should be granted the vote. The guiding principle of his life was opposition to injustice and oppression. 'From early youth,' Pryme wrote, 'he was a friend to Freedom.' At a time when bigotry was rampant, he advocated equal rights for all shades of religious belief and he explained his position with simple logic: 'I do not see why I should deny to others the toleration I claim for myself.' Not such a cold fish, after all!

When Daniel first stood for Parliament, in 1820, he was impelled by duty, not ambition. The cost of the election in Hull only two years before had been so exorbitant that the Whigs had difficulty fielding a candidate. Reluctantly he realised that 'the privacy of domestic life in the country' at Raywell had to be sacrificed.

Hull had two M.P.s, and Daniel and a Tory were elected unopposed. He was 54, he felt he had entered Parliament too late, and he decided to speak only on selected topics: justice and individual liberty were his constant themes. His voice was not strong enough to make him an effective outdoor speaker, but in debate his speeches were 'marked by keen irony and strong, though not ill-natured, sarcasm'.

At the next election, in 1826, he was unenthusiastic for re-election. Duty, however, called once more. An all-party delegation took a petition signed by 1,000 Hull electors to Raywell, begging him to stand, and he replied that he was 'unable to resist'. In a hard-fought fight he kept his seat by a slender margin of 83 votes.

Catholic emancipation was the current, bitterly controversial issue, and Daniel's views on toleration were not popular with his most extreme Protestant supporters. In 1830 he decided not to risk his chances again in Hull but stood successfully for Beverley. Another election was called a year later; his health was noticeably failing and he realised that this was the end of his parliamentary career, though with great courage he campaigned for others.

The rest of the story is melancholy. He withdrew to Raywell and in a rustic temple in the garden he had a plaque erected, inscribed with a verse translated from the Latin, which, very movingly, recorded his anguish at the thought of the final parting from his wife and from Raywell.

Although he had asked for a private funeral, he was held in too high esteem for his wishes to be observed. Over 4,000 people converged on Kirkella Church on the day of his burial in the family vault in 1832 and he was escorted from Raywell by a half-mile cavalcade of carriages and riders. In Hull, Raywell Street was named in his honour.

Raywell is now the property of J. R. Rawson & Sons Ltd. The bay-windowed board room (formerly the drawing room) has views of the peaceful wooded grounds, and the house looks out towards gently rising countryside: a pleasant part of the attractive area to the west of Hull and an ideal setting for the home of Daniel Sykes who was in every sense a gentle man.

Thomas Perronet Thompson
(1783-1869)
Hull's Brilliant but Flawed M.P.

Another very difficult man, easily offended and quick to respond to any sign of slight or disagreement. His parliamentary career was distinctly bumpy but many of his ideas have since come to fruition.

Hull has re-discovered Thomas Perronet Thompson. Everybody knows about William Wilberforce but interest in Thompson has grown only in recent years. When Humberside College of Higher Education (now the University of Humberside) held a competition to name a new lecture theatre in 1984, the winning entry was 'Perronet Thompson', and the opening of the Perronet Thompson School has now made his name part of the local vocabulary.

'Perronet Thompson' sounds far more distinguished than 'Thompson' unadorned, though his father was a no-nonsense Thomas Thompson and the Perronet part was merely a second Christian name (his maternal grandmother's maiden name was Perronet).

Although they became prominent, the Thompsons had a modest beginning. Thomas senior, born in Swine c.1754, had a feckless father who left him to depend on his mother and grandmother. When he was 16 he became a clerk in the Wilberforce family firm; his ability was recognised and he was rapidly promoted and became 'a great man of business', eventually moving into banking as a partner in Smith's Bank. Somehow in his busy life he also found time to be a local historian and author, a Methodist preacher and, from 1807-18, M.P. for Midhurst, Sussex, the first Methodist in the House. Locally he is best remembered for building a Gothic-style mansion at Cottingham in 1816, Cottingham Castle. It was destroyed by fire in 1861, and Castle Hill Hospital later built on the site.

His many activities were exceeded by the wide range of interests energetically pursued by Thomas Perronet, his eldest son, born at the family's Lowgate home in 1783. After receiving his early education at Hull Grammar School under the eminent evangelical head, Rev. Joseph Milner, he went to Queen's College, Cambridge, when he was 15, graduating with high honours when he was still only 18. Yet, instead of following an academic career as might have been expected, he joined

Thomas Perronet Thompson.

Cottingham Castle, 1816, destroyed by fire 1861.

the navy. Even so, in 1804 he was elected a fellow of Queen's College — 'a sort of promotion which has not often gone along with the style and dignity of a midshipman', was his wry comment.

Another odd change of direction was his transfer to the army in 1806, a move which swiftly took him into action and resulted in his capture at Buenos Aires by the Spanish. After release, this brilliant but restless man began yet another phase of his career when, through Wilberforce's influence, he was appointed Governor of Sierra Leone in 1808. The link with Hull now acquired extra significance, for Perronet Thompson was a strenuous opponent of slavery and began to implement the new legislation for the abolition of the slave trade too enthusiastically for the government's liking and he was recalled to England.

Back again with the army, he fought in the Peninsular War but, amazingly, spent his leisure time in camp writing political essays. He was a strange blend of intellectual and man of action and, while campaigning against the French in 1814, he managed to write a treatise on Morals and the Law.

Perronet Thompson then transferred to another regiment bound for India. Though acquitted by a court martial over his personal conduct, he was reprimanded for leading a reckless military expedition, and his active army career ended in 1822 when he returned to England. He was, however, subsequently promoted and finally achieved the rank of General.

But it was not for military exploits that Perronet Thompson is best remembered. He made his mark in the world of politics and political journalism. Articles and pamphlets flowed from his pen on a bizarre assortment of topics, but his masterpiece was a 'Catechism on the Corn Laws' (1824), which went into 18 editions. It sounds an unlikely best-seller, but the great controversy of the day was whether corn should be imported duty-free, and his catechism helped to influence the argument. Perronet Thompson was one of those rare people who are able to write amusingly about economics. Serious points were made in a vigorous style, interspersed with racy humour, and a foretaste of the pamphlet's success was the gale of laughter from the printers setting up the type: when the first edition came out 'the public laughed as the printers had done before them'.

Perronet Thompson became one of the country's leading campaigners for free trade, but his parliamentary career was less successful. He was too much of an individualist to slip easily into the role of popular candidate. Totally fearless, supremely confident of the correctness of his ideas, openly critical of his colleagues, he was not an easy man to work alongside. He had failed to win a seat at Preston in the 1835 general election but a by-election in Hull soon after, caused by the sudden death of a Tory M.P., gave him an opportunity to stand as a Liberal. He was now a nationally famous figure but, like any sensible candidate, he made great play of his other asset, his local birth. 'The whole of my early life was passed in Hull,' he reminded electors. 'Forty years ago I believe I knew almost every man in the street, and every boy and man knew me.' It was the sort of sentimental mush that an audience cheerfully swallows, but, years later, when he had severed his links with Hull, he spoke more candidly about the corruption rampant there: 'If I am asked to say what is the general character of the town, I know, from my recollections of boyhood, that it was as bad as could well be.'

Perronet Thompson was not a handsome man. His face was 'large and somewhat oval-formed' and he was short and stout. His defects, however, made him easily recognisable and, as he went about his canvass, his son, Charles, overheard people asking about the 'little fellow' and encouraging him on with such exhortations as, 'Go to it, old cock!'

Thompson was a Radical, well to the left of the Liberals and much too extreme for many. He was far in advance of public opinion in believing that all men should have the vote — and way beyond most progressive thinkers when he added, 'I really do not know why women should not have it too.'

It was a keenly fought contest and Thompson defeated his Conservative opponent by the narrowest of margins: five votes. The Conservatives then challenged the result, only abandoning the case after a four-day scrutiny costing Thompson an additional £4,000. He never forgave those who caused him this massive, unnecessary expense. 'I have no hesitation in stating my personal conviction that I have been laid down and robbed at the door of the House of Commons,' was his bitter conclusion written 18 years later.

Although a rare speaker, he was a good constituency M.P. and, unlike those candidates who promptly forget their election pledges, he honoured his promises to keep the people of Hull informed about events in Parliament by writing a weekly letter, published in the local press. He was concerned to protect their interests at Westminster but he was unwilling to support any action motivated by humbug or intolerance. When Methodists petitioned in favour of Sunday observance he did not spare their feelings. 'I cannot conceal my opinion that petitions of this nature are likely to produce a directly contrary effect to that desired,' he replied. His recent costly experience made him reluctant to stand again for Hull when a general election was called in 1837. Instead, he tried unsuccessfully at Maidstone. In 1841 he made one last attempt to be elected for Hull, but he was on bad terms with the other Liberal candidate, James Clay, and he came bottom of the poll.

His political career thereafter was decidedly shaky. A whole saga of defeats followed at Marylebone, Manchester and Sunderland before he found a winnable seat at Bradford in 1847. At the next election, in 1852, he was defeated and, when approached as a possible candidate for a Hull by-election, he replied contemptuously that 'he would as soon think of selling his daughter for a concubine in New Orleans'. He became M.P. for Bradford for a final two-year period 1857-9 and made no further attempt to return to the House. He died at his home in Blackheath in 1869.

Thompson is not a man who can be slotted into a neat category. The many facets of his public life are surely indications of a hyperactive brain, constantly gushing with new ideas, but lacking the judgment needed to determine priorities and the self-control which would have enabled him to direct his talents more effectively. The free trade policy for which he campaigned did, however, bring great benefits to 19th-century Britain and his pioneering views on extending the right to vote laid the foundations on which others could build.

By conventional standards he was not a successful man, but Hull is right to give him a belated place of honour. With all his defects, he was a far more admirable character than those who toed a timid party line, and in his independence of outlook and his determination to be true to his deepest convictions he was the sort of M.P. any town should be proud to elect.

Admiral Charles Francis Walker
(1836-1925)

Naval Hero and Beverley Benefactor

I prefer people whose lives cannot be easily explained, whose actions do not fit neatly into a pattern. Admiral Walker was one such, an archetypal Victorian gentleman playing the traditional role of public figure, who set a good example to his equals and made generous gifts to the less privileged. But his early career showed him as a man of action and adventure.

Admiral Walker is the name of a road and — unofficially — of the house which the Admiral occupied for many years. It would be a pity, though, if he survived only as a name, for the man himself was one of Beverley's great characters.

Rear-Admiral Charles Francis Walker, to give him his full title, lived through one of the most significant periods of English history. He was born in 1836, when William IV was on the throne, saw the long reign of Victoria and the shorter one of Edward VII through to their ends and died only in 1925 in his 90th year.

At the time of his birth the Walkers were ascending the social ladder but were still not too far from the days when they were making their money in trade. James Walker was a 17th-century Manchester merchant whose son, another James, moved to Hull, no doubt attracted by the financial prospects in that flourishing port. His country house was at Springhead, then miles from the centre, but now swallowed up by the modern city.

It was his son, yet another James, who in 1802 moved further out of town. As his fortunes rose he took over the fine house in Lairgate, Beverley, then often known as Pennyman House, now The Hall, from the Pennymans, a family of landed gentry which had run into serious debt. This James was the Admiral's grandfather.

Young Charles Frederick left home in January, 1850, at the age of 13, to join the Navy as a midshipman. In his teens he served in the Black Sea during the Crimean War, and for jumping overboard in a heavy sea to rescue an able seaman he was awarded the silver medal of the Royal Humane Society. Promotion came quickly: from sub-lieutenant to lieutenant, then to commander, when he was 28, after distinguishing himself in action against pirates off the China coast. By the time he left the Navy in 1873 when he married Edith Frances Duncombe, the daughter of Admiral the Hon. Charles Duncombe of Kilnwick Percy, he was a captain. In 1888 he was promoted to rear-admiral on the retired list.

The Hall was no longer the main family residence. His father (another James), by now a baronet, had moved further into rural

Rear-Admiral Charles Francis Walker.

The Hall, Lairgate, Beverley: 'Admiral Walker House'.

Yorkshire and purchased a splendid estate at Sand Hutton, but Charles Francis was only a younger son, not the heir to the title and the country seat. Even so, the elegant Beverley house set in beautiful grounds was not a bad consolation prize.

When he took up residence in Beverley, Walker showed himself ready to fill the public role which a gentleman then regarded as the duty attached to privilege. Though never serving on the Council or, like his elder brother, standing for Parliament, he was appointed a J.P., supported the Conservatives and the Church of England, and channelled money into worthy causes. His gifts to the town included reading rooms in Flemingate and Keldgate and a fountain at Beckside, and he established a rifle range (said to be the largest in the country) in the former Temperance Hall. He also gave financial assistance to the Cottage Hospital and to a variety of youth organisations, Scouts, Guides, and Cadets, and, convinced that one day there would be war with Germany, impressed on young men the importance of physical training and shooting. His great friend was the military hero, Lord Roberts — probably one reason why his name was given to the new road opened in 1909.

A contemporary described Walker as 'a man of very generous disposition' and in 1889 the press recorded one of his typical acts of philanthropy: 'By the kindness of Admiral Walker, 60 poor families have been receiving excellent soup every other day (and in some cases every day except Monday) during last week and the present. The soup is made four times a week and is of most nourishing quality.'

The Admiral may have given up his pursuit of pirates but he indulged his love of travel by investing in one of those new-fangled bicycles. Cobbled streets were not conducive to comfortable cycling and, apparently, he paid for a central track to be made down Minster Moorgate so that he could enjoy a smooth ride to and from church.

The conflict with Germany which he had long predicted began in August, 1914, and within three months his elder son had been killed in France. As his particular contribution to the war effort the Admiral kept a herd of Highland cattle on his parkland, and the pastoral scene with 'the rich mellow colouring of the Hall in the background' and the shaggy-coated animals grazing among the 'noble trees' remained a nostalgic memory of old Beverlonians. His younger son, Philip Charles, was Rector of Lockington 1917-1933.

Remarkably, Walker lived to see his father's baronetcy pass to three descendants, his brother, nephew and great-nephew. He was the last private resident of The Hall and in 1926, a year after his death, it was bought by Beverley Borough Council and the park developed for housing and roads.

For Beverley it was the end of an era.

Charles Henry Wilson, Lord Nunburnholme
(1833-1907)
Shipping Magnate and Liberal M.P.

I believe in re-instating people who have been upstaged by their inferiors. C. H. Wilson was a man of many talents, far more important than his better known brother, Arthur, at Tranby Croft. Wilson was a man of great ability and considerable achievement and it is time he was given the limelight he deserves.

Arthur Wilson of Tranby Croft has achieved lasting fame merely by being the unfortunate host to the Prince of Wales when the fateful game of baccarat was played. Yet his elder brother, Charles Henry, who had a distinguished public career and was the real power in the Wilsons' shipping firm after their father retired, is comparatively unknown, even though he brought a hereditary peerage into the family and his statue stands at the Lowgate end of the Guildhall in the city he represented for over 30 years in Parliament.

Born in 1833, the eighth son of Thomas Wilson, he was one of the boys who wore the dashing red-tasselled caps sported by pupils of Kingston College in Beverley Road (now the Kingston Youth Centre), a private Anglican school for the sons of Hull's affluent middle class.

It was a time when there were fortunes to be made by thrusting entrepreneurs like Thomas Wilson. The Town Docks were crowded with shipping and the railway, opened in 1840, linked Hull with the country's major industrial areas and centres of population. Wilson ships started a regular service to foreign ports neglected by other companies, first to Scandinavia and, as the firm progressed, to more wide-spread destinations: Constantinople, the U.S.A., and India. By 1906 a local newspaper was advertising tours to Sweden and St. Petersburg on the *Calypso* and the *Ariosto,* sailing from Hull every Saturday — seven days for £8.12s!

Charles had to begin at the bottom, like other Wilson clerks, but the route to the top was never in doubt. He became a leading figure in Hull's business community as a director of the Hull Dock Company and of the North Eastern Railway Company, and in 1870 he was Sheriff of Hull — an office which required the holder to possess adequate private means to maintain its dignity.

He entered Parliament in 1874 as one of the town's two Liberal

Statue of Charles Henry Wilson, 1st Baron Nunburnholme, outside the Guildhall, Hull.

Warter Priory.

members, transferring to West Hull when the borough was split into divisions in 1885. From a modern political standpoint it may seem odd that Charles Wilson, a wealthy employer, would stand as a Liberal — on the Radical wing, too — particularly as Arthur's son, Stanley, was a Tory M.P. But politics then were not as class-based as they later became, Charles Wilson supported free trade, which had helped Hull to prosper, and many voted for him, irrespective of party labels, attracted by the éclat of the Wilson name, thinking it only right that a man who was such a key figure in the town's economy should represent it at Westminster. The Wilsons, after all, created the largest private shipping company in the world, and some of the glory rubbed off on Hull. In 1885 Charles Wilson obtained the largest majority of any English M.P.

He married in 1871 Florence Wellesley, niece of the Duke of Wellington, and from 1872 the couple made their home at Thwaite House, Cottingham (now the University's Thwaite Hall). The grounds were spacious, and Charles contributed to their delights by landscaping the gardens, constructing a lake, and planting trees. Charles and Florence had one of the typically large families of that period, three sons and four daughters, and, following the example of others who made their money in trade, they showed a determination to raise their social status. Two sons went to Eton, and two daughters married into old-established families: Enid became the Countess of Chesterfield and chatelaine of Benningbrough Hall, and Joan married into one of Yorkshire's most renowned families, the Fairfaxes.

It was, however, Charles himself who set the seal on his own respectability by purchasing a large country estate, and so entering the privileged ranks of the landed gentry. In 1878 he bought Lord Muncaster's mansion, Warter Priory, which stood in a 300-acre estate, and he continued to acquire more land until by the end of the century he owned nearly 8,000 acres in Warter plus more elsewhere. Once again, he set about beautifying the gardens and also making the large house larger still by adding features so highly valued by the Victorians: a baronial-type hall, a marble staircase, and a clock tower. The end result was a massive 100-room residence which later generations saw as 'an unmanageable rambling Victorian monstrosity'. There Charles Wilson lived in lavish style with 22 indoor and 40 outdoor servants.

For him Warter Priory had one minor disadvantage: it was a little too far out of Hull for easy commuting, and so, in 1897, he had another house built, in Thwaite Street, Cottingham. Though only a modest *pied-à-terre* by Wilson standards, it was a far more substantial house than its original name, 'The Bungalow', suggests. Now renamed Cleminson Hall (another University property), it still retains fireplaces carved with his monogram, 'CHW', a proud mark of ownership, and with assorted nautical symbols. Most splendid of all, though, is the bathroom, a perfect period piece equipped with the mod. cons. of nearly a century ago.

Charles Wilson had, of course, a London house, in fashionable Grosvenor Square, and he was also a member of the Reform Club. In Parliament he was regarded as an authority on shipping and commercial subjects, and on one of the great political issues which remains unsolved he followed Gladstone's advocacy of Home Rule for Ireland.

In Hull, however, his reputation as a Radical was badly damaged by a dock strike in 1893. Unemployment was rising, dockers were employed on a casual basis, and Wilson decided to rejoin the Shipping Federation which gave preference to non-union men. There was a bitter six-week conflict, police were drafted in from out of town, the strikers capitulated, and in the 1895 General Election Wilson was opposed by Tom McCarthy, Hull's first Labour candidate. The strike left an aftermath of recrimination but Wilson still defeated McCarthy by a massive 6,637 votes to 1,400.

Then came an even greater triumph for the House of Wilson. In 1906 Charles was raised to the peerage and took the sonorous title, Lord Nunburnholme: disrespectful snipers muttered that he could hardly call himself Lord Warter in view of the source of the family wealth. Soon after his enoblement he spoke in the Lords on a topic which had roused considerable emotion in Hull, the North Sea Outrage of 1904 when the Russians accidentally fired on a British fishing fleet. Only

The Saloon, Warter Priory.

three years later there were understandable protests when it was announced that Royal Navy ships were to visit Russian ports. Lord Nunburnholme told his fellow peers that feeling had been high in Hull at the time of the incident but it had now very much subsided: 'The fishermen generally had not joined in this desire to perpetuate the memory of that outrage. It was a very terrible one, but I quite agree that the matter should now be allowed to rest.' Lord Nunburnholme lived to enjoy his elevated status for only a year. His eldest son, Charles Henry Wellesley Wilson, who had succeeded him as M.P. for West Hull, now quickly moved into the Lords and his younger brother, Guy, took over the seat. Not surprisingly, there were Liberals who felt aggrieved that West Hull was regarded as a 'Wilson fief'.

The Warter estate was sold to the Vesteys in 1928 and to the Guinness Trust in 1968. Many local people have vivid memories of visiting Warter Priory when the great auction of the house's contents took place the following year. The house itself was later demolished. Earlier the bodies of Lord Nunburnholme and his family had been removed from what was intended to be their last resting place on their estate and reburied one dark depressing day in a secluded corner of the churchyard at Warter.

It is a peaceful spot, but the time has come for the man himself to be given his rightful place of honour in the history of East Yorkshire.

The Bungalow, Cottingham, now Cleminson Hall.